D0743823

SONG *of the* WEST

SELECTED POEMS OF
GEORG TRAKL

Translated with an Introduction by
ROBERT FIRMAGE

NORTH POINT PRESS
San Francisco   1988

English translation and Introduction
   copyright © 1988 by Robert Firmage
Printed in the United States of America
Library of Congress Catalogue Card Number: 88-61179
ISBN: 0-86547-352-8 (cloth), 0-86547-353-6 (paper)

Contents

Translator's Introduction

This volume is in commemoration of the centennial of the birth of the Austrian poet Georg Trakl. Of the major European poets of this century, Trakl remains among the most underappreciated in America. Where he is known, his notoriety too often takes the form of a summary concatenation of the more lurid details of his biography, by virtue of which he is seen as a kind of Teutonic Rimbaud, a *poète maudit* of death, drugs, and madness, whose voice of synesthesia and despair serves as a witness to the failure of the will attendant on the collapse of the Hapsburg Empire. But this characterization, which would otherwise seem such as to foster his enduring celebrity, has not proven sufficient to dispel the obscurity of his writing. In the words of his editor, Walther Killy, "the language of this poet is dark."[1]

Such darkness has had the effect of rendering Trakl's work opaque both to translation and to interpretation. Although interest in that work has recently revived under the impetus of James Wright and Robert Bly, translations of his poems in America have been few and have gone largely unnoticed. This is all the more striking in view of the great success recently accorded to translations of his near-contemporary, the Prague-born Rainer Maria Rilke. Considering that Trakl's influence on twentieth-century German poetry has probably exceeded that of Rilke, America is confronted with the phenomenon of a poet whose reputation reaches farther than his voice.

Interpretations of that voice have ranged from the visionary (Trakl as Christian ecstatic) to the clinical (Trakl as psychotic). Though these interpretations start from details of the poet's life, and from the seemingly more accessible aspects of his writing, most may be said to offer little in the way of an overview of his work as a whole. His definitive biography has yet to be written. Thus, even in German-speaking countries, Trakl remains an enigma. Since in America he remains an enigma wrapped in silence, this volume seeks at least to break that silence by providing new translations of his strongest work. That the enigma will abide seems ineluctable, for it is wrought of an intertwining of a life of strangest fascination and a work of febrile darkness, which serve both to obscure and clarify each other.

Georg Trakl was born on February 3, 1887, the fourth of six surviving children, in Salzburg, Austria. His father, Tobias, was what we might call a "self-made man," having risen from humble origins to a position of social prominence through unstinting devotion to his hardware business. After the death of his first wife, he married Maria Halik, who, although a Catholic, had divorced her husband to marry him, giving birth to their first child three months before their wedding. Tobias found himself in a position to provide his growing family with a large house in one of the best neighborhoods of Salzburg, and to hire a governess for his children, who taught them to converse among themselves in French, to play the piano, and to enjoy the many cultural institutions of the city of Mozart's birth. The children are said to have lacked nothing in the way of material goods or social esteem, but they may not have been so fortunate in regard to parental affection. Tobias seems to have been more interested in his business than in his family, and of Maria it is reported that she was addicted to opium and subject to long bouts of "depression," that she took more pleasure in her china collection than in the raising of her children. It is in this familial situation, outwardly "normal" or even exemplary, that many commentators have seen the seeds of the poet's later "madness."

Two often-recounted incidents from Trakl's childhood have been said to provide evidence of his early "abnormality." As a very young child he is reported to have thrown himself in the path of a running horse. He is also said to have attempted, unsuccessfully, to throw himself in the tracks of a moving locomotive. But an even more striking witness to some seeming childhood "death wish" is the story of his attempt, somewhat later, to walk into a lake. He succeeded in getting far enough, before he was noticed, fully to submerge himself in its waters, and it was only the position of his hat, floating on the surface, that enabled rescuers to find him before he drowned.

Whatever the significance of these incidents, by early adolescence Trakl had assumed behavior that was seen by his townsmen as distinctly "abnormal." Introduced to narcotics by the son of a neighboring pharmacist, he is said to have become a habitual user of chloroform and of cigarettes dipped in opium before he was fourteen. He is also said to have frequented brothels, worn "strange" clothes, and been fascinated with suicide. He failed his fourth year of secondary school, had to repeat it, and finally dropped out of school altogether upon failing his seventh year.

Even for one leery of psychological schools of literary criticism, it would be difficult to gainsay the significance of the "family romance" in Trakl's work. It has often been remarked that Trakl's writings are autobiographical, at least to the extent that the figures of the "father," the "mother," and the "sister," recurrent throughout his poems, reflect beyond the possibility of coincidence what we know of his relationship with his own family. His feelings about his father seem to have been cool, at times almost contemptuous, yet not unmixed with a certain distant veneration. Of his mother he is reported to have confessed that at times he hated her so much that he could have murdered her with his own hands. But whatever was lacking in his relationship with his parents was clearly compensated by his deep love for his sister.

Margarete Trakl was born five years later than Georg, but became his boon companion through his childhood and adolescence, as well as the only woman to whom he seems ever to have formed a close attachment. It is probably not an exaggeration to claim that she was the love of his life. He once remarked that she was "the most beautiful girl, the greatest artist and the strangest woman" he had ever known.[2] The psychiatrist Theodor Spoerri claimed to have found incontrovertible evidence that there had been an incestuous relationship between the two, but refused to divulge his sources out of consideration for the persons still living.[3] Whatever the truth of his contention, it is undeniable that incest is a major motif in Trakl's poetry, where it assumes the significance of an archetypal fall from grace. Grete's later life proved fully as ill-starred as her brother's. She was an accomplished pianist, but, like Georg, formed an early dependence on drugs, and, after an unhappy marriage and a near-fatal miscarriage in 1914, took her own life at a party in Berlin in 1917.

After dropping out of school, Trakl decided on a career in pharmacy, perhaps, as is often suggested, in order to facilitate his acquisition of drugs. He spent three years of conscientious apprenticeship at the White Angel Pharmacy in Salzburg, and then moved to Vienna in 1908 in order to complete his degree, which was awarded in 1910. It was during this time that his earliest poetic activity began. From 1904 to 1906 he had been a member of an adolescent literary club in Salzburg, for which he wrote numerous poems, and through which he became acquainted with the work of Nietzsche and Dostoievski, as well as Baudelaire, Verlaine, George, and von Hofmannsthal. In 1906 he began writing prose sketches and book reviews for the local papers, and had two plays, *Totentag* and *Fata Morgana* (both of which he later burned), performed locally, under the patronage of Salzburg's own *poète maudit*, Gustav Streicher. The first was a qualified success, but the second was almost universally panned, and although he worked on two more plays between 1908 and 1910, he seems thereafter to have devoted most of his energy to lyric poetry. Streicher is credited with an influence on Trakl beyond theatrical patronage, since at this time Trakl began to wear "dandified clothes" and long hair, and to spend hours at a time drinking wine in brothels and country taverns.

In Salzburg and Vienna, Trakl wrote many poems, a selection of which was made by his friend Erhard Buschbeck, in an attempt to interest publishers in Trakl's work. Buschbeck's success was limited, however, to the publication of a few of Trakl's poems in the prestigious *Neue Wiener Journal*, and it was not until 1939 that the collection was finally published by Buschbeck, under the title *Aus goldenem Kelch*.

In 1910 Trakl was drafted for one year of compulsory military duty, and in 1911 returned to Salzburg to work in the White Angel. But he found himself unable to deal with the public; it is said that one morning he sweated through six different changes of shirts. He soon reenlisted in the army and joined a regiment at Innsbruck in April 1912. It was there that he met the man who was to be his mainstay for the rest of his life. Ludwig von Ficker, seven years older than Trakl, was editor of *Der Brenner*, a semi-monthly journal devoted to what has been described as an early form of "Christian existentialism" (pioneering, for instance, the revival of Kierkegaard), and which Karl Kraus once called the only honest periodical in Austria. At the time of their meeting, von Ficker had already published one of Trakl's poems, and a spontaneous friendship seems to have arisen between them. Von Ficker provided Trakl with psychological, financial, and emotional support, and offered him, as well, a forum for his writing. What Trakl gave von Ficker is less clear, but it is unquestionable that von Ficker had a genuine and profound respect for Trakl's genius and a love for his character, which he retained until his death in the 1960s.

Trakl was no happier with army life than with the life of a pharmacist. In a letter to Buschbeck he characterizes his lot at Innsbruck as a life

> in the most brutal and sordid city . . . that exists on this overladen and accursed world. And when I think that an alien will may leave me suffering here for as much as a decade, I feel like collapsing in a teary convulsion of inconsolable hopelessness. What does it matter. After all, I will always remain a poor Kaspar Hauser.[4]

After a fight with an officer who had reprimanded him for spitting on the floor, he requested and received reserve status in November 1912.

For the rest of his life he was unable to find steady employment. More precisely, although he received two government positions, he found working at them unbearable, and resigned from the first after two hours, the second after two months. Until the beginning of the war, he spent most of his time either in Salzburg or in Innsbruck, where he lived at the house of von Ficker, writing poetry and making desultory attempts to find employment, sometimes (perhaps after the model of Rimbaud) in exotic places such as Borneo. It may well have been his poetry that rendered employment impossible. From his first meeting with von Ficker to his death was the period of his most intense creativity, during which he wrote the poems on which his reputation rests, and from which most of the poems of this volume have been selected. His major breakthrough occurred immediately upon leaving the army, in December 1912, through work on the poem "Helian," which he called the "most precious and painful" he had ever written.[5] It was completed in January 1913 and was immediately hailed by von Ficker and by Karl Borromaeus Heinrich, an Austrian critic associated with the *Brenner* circle, as a "German classic." In April 1913 Kurt Wolff, the publisher usually credited with the "discovery" of Kafka, wrote Trakl for permission to publish a small edition of his poems in Wolff's series *Der jüngste Tag*. In July 1913, after some wrangling between poet and publisher as to the scope and contents of the book, *Gedichte* appeared as a compromise, a volume primarily of rhymed poems, part of whose selction is said to have been made by Franz Werfel. It seems that Trakl was not entirely satisfied with it, for he began at once to work on a second volume, *Sebastian im Traum*, which he completed before the war, but which Wolff was unable to publish until after the poet's death.

In August 1914, at the outbreak of World War I, Trakl's reserve unit was activated and sent to the province of Galicia in Poland, where the Austrians prepared to meet the Russians' advance. The armies met in the battle of Grodek, and the Austrians were routed. In the aftermath, they found themselves in such disarray that Trakl, although nominally a pharmacist, was commanded to care for ninety severely wounded men, who had been hospitalized in a barn. Lacking all means to alleviate their distress, Trakl was driven to a state of frenzy by their suffering, which reached its climax, as the story is told, in a scenario of surrealistic intensity. One of the wounded, unable to bear his pain any longer, shot himself in the head, and Trakl, rushing in at the sound of gunfire, was greeted by the sight of pieces of the victim's brain sticking to the wall. Distraught, he rushed back outside, only to be confronted by the apparition of corpses dangling from a row of bare trees—local peasants, hanged on suspicion of disloyalty to the Austrians. He stormed in upon a group of officers at lunch, declared his intention to shoot himself, and was finally restrained only by physical force. He was soon sent to Krakow for psychological evaluation, where he was placed in a prison cell with a soldier suffering from a severe case of delirium tremens. The preliminary diagnosis of the army psychiatrists was that Trakl was a victim of "dementia praecox," but they were unable to complete their investigation. On November 4, 1914, Trakl died, after spending one day in a coma, of an overdose of cocaine.

It has long been disputed whether Trakl intended to commit suicide or died accidently. The question will no doubt remain forever unanswered. The case is the same in regard to the issue of Trakl's alleged "psychosis." That his behavior was sometimes erratic cannot be denied, and it is likewise true that during his entire adult life he was subject to alcoholism, various drug addictions, and attendant trancelike "visionary" states. But such considerations would seem to have but little bearing on the quality of his writing, which is certainly a great deal more than a symptom of derangement. Whatever the state of his mental health, about which he himself at times expressed concern, it thus behooves us to take seriously his own account: that it was the consequence of his attempt "to give to the truth what belongs to the truth." [6] A precondition of such an attempt, Trakl found, was the need to submit without reservation to the details of his own psychological experience. It is in his letters that we most clearly catch glimpses of a soul overwhelmed by the consequences of such unconditional openness. For instance, in 1908 he writes to his sister Minna:

> I believe it must be terrible to live always in full consciousness of all the animal instincts which constantly whirl through life. I have experienced, smelled, touched the most frightening possibilities within myself, have heard the demons howling in my blood, the thousand devils which drive the flesh mad with their spurs. What a horrible nightmare!
> Gone! Today this vision of reality has again sunk into nothing . . . and I, all living ear, listen again to the melodies within me, and my winged eye dreams again its images, which are more beautiful than all reality. [7]

We are struck by the uncanny rapid alternation of the horrible with the sublime in this passage, an alternation characteristic also of his poetry as a whole. To him it seemed that the portrayal of "truth" demanded that he subordinate himself to two extreme poles of the same "reality," in order to bring to speech some aspect of their greater unity. This unity he found, to employ a word recurring throughout his poems, "unspeakable."

> . . . I am oppressed by all too much (what an infernal chaos of rhythms and images!) to find time for anything else but to give it only the most minimal of shape, [and] finally to see myself, before that which cannot be mastered, as a laughable bungler, whom the slightest external impetus sends into convulsions and delirium.[8]

In this endeavor Trakl was not without antecedents. It was Nietzsche who warned us of the madness implicit in the artist's attempt to discover the ground of reality. But its ultimate cost is perhaps measured by the agony expressed in the following letter to von Ficker in 1914.

> It is a nameless unhappiness when one's world breaks in two. O my God, what a judgment has broken upon me. Tell me that I must have the strength to stay alive and to do what is true. Tell me that I am not mad. A stony darkness has broken upon me.[9]

This outcry records only one of the several crises besetting the life of the poet. But it seems that out of them his poetry was achieved.

Trakl's effect on others seems on the whole to have been enigmatic. Hans Limbach, for instance, remarks on his "uncommonly dignified" appearance, yet notes as well that "a dark, almost evil feature gave him a criminal-like fascination."[10] One of the fullest (and most sympathetic) portraits of his character is provided by von Ficker.

> He found his way in external life ever more difficult, while the fountain of his poetic creativity opened ever deeper. . . . He, who was a heavy drinker and drug user, never lost his noble, uncommonly tempered intellectual self-control; there was no one who ever saw him so much as sway or grow impertinent in a condition of drunkenness, although his manner of speaking, otherwise so mild and as

though circling about an unutterable muteness, could often harden curiously over wine in the advanced hours of the night, and sharpen into scintillating anger. . . . In general, he was a silent, taciturn, but in no way aloof person; on the contrary, he could get along with simple, unaffected people, insofar as they had their hearts "in the right place"—and especially with children—in the kindest and most human manner.[11]

Many acquaintances have mentioned his tendency to sit unspeaking in their presence for hours at a time, then suddenly to launch into a monologue as cryptic as his silence. A remark once made to Theodor Däubler may serve as an example: "We fall into an inapprehensible darkness. How could dying, the moment which leads to eternity, ever be short?"[12]

Such earnestness has no doubt been a factor in leading several critics to treat Trakl as a Christian poet. Although his mother was a Catholic, and he attended a Catholic school, Trakl was raised a Protestant, the faith of his father. He remained indifferent to creed and dogma after his youth, but there are several reasons for thinking that, unlike Rilke, he never broke entirely from a Christian, and indeed somewhat Catholic, worldview. His poetry is steeped in Christian symbols and motifs (fall and redemption, bread and wine, the good shepherd, the fisherman). A religious consciousness seems to have extended into his daily life as well; in 1961 von Ficker is reported to have remarked: "What I know of Christianity I owe to Trakl."[13] But it would be a mistake to see in Trakl's work a reflection of Christian orthodoxy. His use of Christian symbolism is not only highly idiosyncratic, but seems unconcerned with accepted dogma, and, if traced in detail, would probably reveal a "Christianity" at least as radical as that of William Blake. Counterbalancing this Christian symbolism is a strain of "pagan" motifs reminiscent of, and in part derived from, Hölderlin. The most certain aspects of his belief can perhaps best be summarized by quoting his two published "aphorisms." The "Christian" element is captured in the first of these: "Feeling in moments of deathlike existence: All men are worthy of love. Waking you feel the bitterness of the world; within it is all your unredeemed guilt; your poem an imperfect atonement." Nonetheless, in view of his sense of the unmitigated evil of the world, his thought could equally be said to bear affinity to Gnosticism. Although such a view will not be argued here, it is at least supported by the second aphorism: "Only to him, who despises happiness, comes knowledge." Such "knowledge," we may expect, is not unconnected with his quest for the "truth," the expression of which is the main goal of his poetry.

In terms of this goal, religion represents for Trakl a sensibility, or way of life, that has become inaccessible to modern man. In one of his letters he said of his work that it is "an all too faithful mirror of a godless, accursed century."[14] The significance of this remark lies largely in the historical consciousness that it shares with his poetry as a whole. Although he is not concerned, like Blake, that his work should body forth a full-scale mythology, it remains mythological in its essence, for its concern is to present the myth, or story, of the continuity between the present state of man and earlier states, in which his relation to "ultimate truth" was both simpler and happier. Thus it could be said that the theme of his poetry is the natural history of the soul. Seen from a less personal and religious perspective, it could equally be said that his theme is precisely the "decline of the West."

Oswald Spengler conceived his magnum opus before the outbreak of World War I, wrote most of it during that conflict, and published it soon after. He gave it the title *Untergang des Abendlands* without cognizance, so far as I know, of Trakl's poetry. It is assuredly the case that Trakl's repeated use, often in close proximity, of the words "Untergang" and "Abendland" is not to be explained by reference to Spengler. Yet something very close to Spengler's thesis, that Western civilization is in a state of inexorable decline from its period of flower in earlier centuries, is undeniably a major theme of Trakl's later work. It is beyond the scope of this essay to analyze the reasons for such a coincidence, though it is no doubt at least partly to be explained in terms of the influence of Nietzsche on both Trakl and Spengler. Although Trakl's view can hardly be called a thesis, since it is not developed discursively, it seems to embrace two convictions worthy of our notice. The first is that Western culture attained its zenith in the so-called

Dark Ages, which were for Trakl preeminently an age of faith, from which contemporary men have fallen precipitously into ruin. The second is that the urbanization of the nineteenth and twentieth centuries is the major cause and symbol of this fall from grace. Trakl's theme, with its dual emphasis on faith and nature, the Christian and the pagan, is developed from an individual rather than from a sociological perspective. It is the individual, the "solitary grandchild," who suffers the effects of this fall, while darkly foreseeing a still darker future, and whose only recourse seems to be his suffering and, wherever possible, his love. Especially in "Helian" and "Sebastian Dreaming," the fall of man is recapitulated in the fall of an individual, through the process of his maturation, of his acculturation into this "godless century," into a state of isolation, "derangement," and despair. It is the natural history of the soul to descend from the innocence and faith of childhood to the corruption and melancholy of adulthood, to come to participate in an evil it is powerless to change. But this evil must be recognized as a social evil; the fall of the individual comes through his need to participate in the ways of his fallen culture. Nevertheless, the darkness of the sensibility and language of this poet are not always unrelieved by hints of light. The bleakness of the fallen soul is sometimes redeemed by "rosy choirs" of resurrection, or by the "blue" and "green" and "gold" of nature. Through his ability to love, through his communion with the pristine purity of springtime, the "lonely one" at times views darkly the promise of a brighter end.

A combination of Romanticism and Christian eschatology is not unique to Trakl, but the identification of the natural with the divine, of the social with the evil, is probably as pronounced in his work as in that of any poet since Rousseau. The affinity of his poems with those of certain of his German contemporaries, such as Heym, Benn, and Lichtenberg, soon to be lumped together with him under the label "Expressionists," was remarked almost immediately upon their publication. But, whereas most of the Expressionists derived their inspiration from the great industrial centers of Protestant northern Germany, and hence express an alienation whose starkness most often admits of no solution short of doomsday, Trakl's poems reflect the still largely rural landscapes of Catholic Austria, where industrialization was more a trend than a fait accompli, and whose cities were still more notable for the detritus of past glories and the gilded splendors of contemporary culture than for urban blight. Thus, although Trakl is hardly oblivious to the threat of industrialization and its "toppling cities of steel," his main focus remains on civilization itself, with its consequent alienation from faith and nature. It is in part owing to their reactionary focus on the conflict between past and future, to their concern with "truth," that his poems tend to possess a richer texture than the stark manifestos of his northern contemporaries, and have tended as well to have a commensurately greater influence on the work of his successors. Instead of satires on mankind, seen from a God's (or Devil's) eye view, Trakl offers the perspective of an individual caught in a conflict of competing darknesses from which he cannot escape. Like Kafka, Trakl presents us with the modern individual, in all his anguish and ambiguity.

But Trakl's affinity with the Expressionists is not merely a matter of their common concern with doom. As Walter H. Sokel explains, from a formal perspective his writing is also expressionistic.

> Trakl represents in Expressionist poetry an equivalent to Kandinsky's role in Expressionist painting. Just as Kandinsky creates pure compositions of colors and lines, so Trakl creates pure compositions of autonomous metaphors. . . . Each metaphor has a more-or-less definite emotional tonality and combines with the other metaphors of which the poem consists not in a conceptually coherent sequence of thoughts, but in an incoherent stream of images. . . .
>
> Yet each poem has an inner coherence, not the coherence of logical thought, but of a musical composition. . . . The metaphoric image acts somewhat like a note in a musical score indicating that a certain tone or chord is to be played. Or it can be compared to a shade of color in an Expressionist painting, which does not describe the object to which it may be attached, but designates a certain mood which the painter wishes to convey.[15]

Although such an analysis is not without its merits, it does not go far enough in explaining why Trakl's "compositions" work so well, what gives them their "musical" or "emotional" coherence. A formalist approach to Trakl's poetry leaves out the significance of his own avowal of commitment to "truth." Given that his poems work like Expressionist paintings, the real question is why he (and other Expressionists) have chosen this means to convey "what is to be portrayed." Especially since he (like the others) seems so concerned with doom, with the fall of man, it is to be wondered whether such a theme demands such a treatment. What precisely do Trakl's poems express through their "incoherent streams of images"?

There are many who would deny that they express anything thereby, who would claim that they are instead merely symptoms of derangement. Such a perspective is exemplified by Michael Francis Sharp, who sees in Trakl's "madness" the key to an understanding of the "strength" of his poetry.

> For its effectiveness—the intensity of the effect it exercises— depends largely on the degree to which it can "infect" or inculcate the reader with its optics and structures. A decrease in distance from the altered perspectives of experience in the madness of Trakl brings with it an increase of understanding.[16]

Insofar as it suggests that one must oneself become "infected with madness" to understand his writings, such a position would seem to represent a last recourse in the interpretation of Trakl. For part of what Trakl suggests is that it is our civilization, our sense of "logical coherence," that is truly mad. Nonetheless, what seems to me right about Sharp's analysis is the suggestion that we need to allow ourselves to be "infected" with Trakl's perspective in order truly to comprehend what his poems are saying. However, if this is to be effective, we must not prejudge whether we are being infected with madness or with sanity, nor even, if it indeed be madness, whether it is pathological or divine.

Trakl's poetic genius resides preeminently in the techniques and perfection of his verse. In letters written to von Ficker and to Buschbeck in 1915 and in 1917, Rilke was perhaps the first to recognize the merit of Trakl's poems in terms of their contribution to the art of poetry.

> In the meantime I have . . . read much in them: overwhelmed, astonished, wondering and perplexed; for one soon comprehends that the conditions of these rising and fading tones are irretrievably singular, like the circumstances from which a dream might arise. I imagine that even one who stands nearby must experience these vistas and insights as though pressed, an exile, against a pane of glass: for Trakl's life passes as in mirror-images and fills its entire space, which cannot be entered, like the space in a mirror.[17]

> For me the Trakl poem is an object of sublime existence. But now it first confounds me how its form, fleeting from the first and lightly bypassed in its description, was in a position to display the weight of its perpetual oblivion in such exact images. It occurs to me that this entire work has its likeness in the dying of Li Po: here as there is falling the pretext for inexorable ascension.
>   In the history of the poem Trakl's books are important contributions toward the liberation of the poetic figure. In them a new dimension of spiritual space seems to be measured out and the emotional-material prejudice to be refuted: that in the direction of lament only lament is to be found—for there as well is world.[18]

These passages are remarkable not only for the way in which they prefigure Rilke's own subsequent use of the motifs of mirror, space, lament, and rising/falling, especially in the *Duino Elegies* and the *Sonnets to Orpheus*, but also for their insight on the precision of Trakl's language. Far from an "incoherent stream of images," Trakl's poems serve to define a "space" in which his figures, in Rilke's parlance, are "liberated" from the demands of reference to the world of quotidian existence. Instead, they act to create, by means of their mutual interactions, a "new dimension" of space, which is free for the investment, not of the rationalization characteristic of modern views of "reality," but rather of an affective consciousness too often lacking in such rationalization. It is precisely such consciousness that is the means to the "truth" Trakl seeks.

One of the most readily noted features of his practice is synesthesia, the displacement of epithets from one realm of sensory experience onto images from another realm. Thus it is common to find phrases in his poems such as "ein blaues Wild" (a blue deer) or "tönendes Gold" (ringing gold). But such displacement in Trakl goes beyond sensory experience. For instance, he also often displaces emotional epithets, such as "traurig" (sorrowful) or "einsam" (lonely) onto inanimate objects. The shock occasioned by such displacement often serves to invest his symbols with an affective sense that seems to displace the entire image-complex into a different world. The "spirituality" of this world, noted by Rilke, is underwritten in Trakl's practice by a final displacement—that of terms such as "heilig" (holy), "geistig" (spiritual), and "Engel" (angel) onto the image-complexes. It is in this way that Trakl seems to share in an oft-noted characteristic of modern poetry—the rejection of mimesis. The poem is no longer a mirror of the world of nature, but rather a world unto itself, a world created by its own words.

In the case of Trakl, however, it must be stressed that the world of the poem, although "irreal" in the sense of being thus "displaced" from the "real" world, is in no sense completely liberated from the demands of mimesis. Trakl's "blue world" is at once an artificial world, "seen through a glass darkly," and our world, seen from some undefined extrapersonal vantage, which threatens always to dissolve into the unreal, but counterbalances this tendency by the uncanny exactness of its images, by the rightness of its perspective. The whole point of Trakl's endeavor is to mirror the deeper aspects of human experience. In this respect, Trakl's practice differs considerably from that of other modern poets such as Yeats and Valéry. The aspect of "artifice" is deemphasized in Trakl's work, in favor of the notion of an underlying, extrapersonal reality. The "poetic figure," while liberated from the stricter demands of mimesis, nonetheless participates in a new mimetic relation to the world. It is Salzburg or Innsbruck or Grodek that is being described in each poem: only the perspective is "artificial."

In order to understand the reason for this, we must return to Trakl's confrontation with the "two faces of reality." Killy provides us with crucial insight in a discussion of Trakl's typical method of composition.

> When we decipher the moving, often endlessly varied manuscripts, scribbled on old letters, coffeehouse menus, envelopes, and notebook pages, we encounter again and again passages such as the following: ". . . a smile full of sorrow and humility has petrified your countenance." However, this address to himself in "Winter Night" did not read this way from the beginning. At first the poet had written, " . . . a smile full of sorrow and arrogance has petrified your countenance." Then he replaced "arrogance" immediately with its opposite, "humility," considered anew, restored "arrogance" again, crossed it out once more, and in its place put "shame." This word he also exchanged for its opposite, and from it made "a smile full of sorrow and pride." Finally he returned in the manuscript to the expression "sorrow and humility," which was transformed once more, in a final decision over the galley proofs, to "arrogance," the definitive version.[19]

Killy sees the motive force behind this extreme flip-flop from one concept to its opposite to be Trakl's concern not so much with the individual elements of each poem as with the poem as a whole, and, in particular, with what Killy terms its "ground-attunement." As he explains, Trakl

> once used the word "valence" for this ground-attunement. "Gold" is such a value, whether it belongs to the sinking skiff or itself comes, ringing, into appearance. The "withered tree" is another, and the presentation of the process of withering is more important to the poet than that of each subordinated phenomenon. These are modifiable and are oriented less toward reality than toward the flow of images, tones, and relations in the whole of the poem.[20]

Trakl's perspective thus escapes the demands of mimesis insofar as it subordinates the details of his experience, the individual elements of the poem, to the "truth" of his experience as a whole, to the "ground-attunement" of those elements. But what, we might ask, is the nature of such "attunement"? Killy answers only that, in attempting verbally to resolve the tension between the unspeakableness of his experience and the need to understand it, Trakl adopted the "most ancient" means of poetry—"enigmatic speech"—in which "the mystery remains alive."[21]

Yet more deserves to be said about this attempt. I have suggested that Trakl's work remains mimetic, but that the "reality" that it "mirrors" is not the world of quotidian experience. Neither is it the world of the subjective, emotional responses of the poet. The "mimesis" of which I speak is secured through the attainment of a perspective that, although extrapersonal in the sense of being detached from the concerns of an individual ego, and hence from the concerns of the society in which he is nurtured, remains the achievement of a single individual in ultimate confrontation with the most basic aspects of his existence. It is the achievement, to use a word favored by Trakl, of the soul. To become "infected" by Trakl's methods of expression is to learn to apprehend reality at a level deeper than the rational, and rationalizing, structures of the socialized ego. It is to see the world *ab novo*, with the eyes of an Adam, the eyes of a Kaspar Hauser. It is to attain to a level of apperception in which the dual mysteries of one's own existence as a finite isolated being, and of the ineluctable givenness of the world as what Yeats has termed "the body of Fate," are perceived afresh and merge into a single mystery, the central datum of experience, which "convulses the breast of the stranger."

What must be achieved is no less than a breakdown of rationality itself. But, since language is preeminently both the medium of rationality and a principal means of its reinforcement, Trakl must employ his language in such a way that it subverts at least part of its own essence. To further such an aim, he characteristically employs a strategy, of which the displacement mentioned above is an aspect, involving a systematic distortion of diction and syntax. This has the dual effect of thwarting the reader's conditioned expectations and of rendering many passages of his poems virtually opaque to translation or to interpretation.

By means of the "displacement of the poetic figure," through synesthesia and the placing of primitive perceptual ("blue," "icy"), elemental ("stone," "water"), and emotional epithets into contexts that seem at first to refuse them, Trakl disrupts the common rational associations between words in favor of juxtapositions that startle the reader into a fresh apprehension of the meaning of these words in isolation. The weighting of his language in favor of emotional and perceptual characteristics is not accidental, for it is precisely these characteristics which seem to arise from a level of human apprehension more fundamental than rationality. It is as if one is being invited to return to the pristine signification of one's most basic vocabulary, and to use it to construct a new ordering of reality. Put differently, one is invited to perceive and to feel the world that one has heretofore taken for granted in a manner divorced from one's prior conceptions of the nature of that world.

Such a method is limited, however, by a feature intrinsic to our use of words: it is impossible entirely to divorce our rationalizing associations from any given usage. Trakl cannot create a wholly new vocabulary, a pristine language, but must content himself with an attempt to choose a vocabulary as free as possible from such associations. To aid in this process, he employs several characteristic idiosyncrasies.

Trakl's diction is notable for its repeated use of the same expressions. Several epithets, recurring constantly, such as "blau" (blue), "dunkel" (dark), and "still" (silent), seem to serve as motifs about which his other expressions are constellated. They thus act as the means whereby the "ground-attunement" of the poem is secured. That is to say, through their reiteration they establish an "atmosphere," which works primarily on an emotional level, and which suffuses each poem as a whole, thereby "coloring" their neighboring expressions with their "valence." Trakl's poems breathe a blue and silent darkness, whose effect on the reader is such as to instill a sense of the world peculiar to his poetry, and thus to help to define the sense of the psychic states to which he also constantly refers, such as "melancholy," "guilt," and "sorrow." Likewise, the reiteration of various terms for birds and trees, for hills and ponds, peoples his "soulscapes" with the objects of nature, seen through the lens of his primal motifs. An example of the interplay between the emotional and "objective" aspects of his terms is provided by his frequent use of the term "Wild" to refer to non-domestic animals, presumably deer. "Wild," however, is primarily a hunting term, corresponding to the English "game," and thus bears the connotation of victimization of innocence, of something born to be destroyed. By preferring this term to its possible equivalents, Trakl focuses on a particular aspect of nature in juxtapostion to society, which is further reinforced by similar choices. This example also illustrates a typical problem in translating Trakl: the best English equivalent possessing both the connotation and objective reference of "Wild" (without engendering the unwanted ambiguity inherent in "game") is "prey," which is neither as common nor as specific as the German term.

But there are times when ambiguity plays a major role in Trakl's poetry. An example is his frequent use of "Geschlecht," which can mean "sex," "race," "family," or "generation." Thus, in "Helian," when he says, "Erschütternd ist der Untergang des Geschlechts," this seems to mean, simultaneously, that the fall (or decline) of sexuality, of Western culture, of a particular family, and of a particular generation, is shattering. There is no term in English with this full range of signification. I have thus had to content myself with "generation," though at times I have used "flesh" instead.

One of my reasons for this choice introduces another characteristic of Trakl's diction: his frequent use of archaism, often with terms having a distinct biblical "flavor." A good example is his preference for "Antlitz" over the more usual "Gesicht" to denote a face. I have followed this usage by rendering "Antlitz" as "countenance" wherever possible. This has the effect of creating a context that is "elevated" and reactionary: the reader must respond to a vocabulary of faith rather than to the "flatter" parlance of contemporary culture. This is reinforced by Trakl's frequent employment of religious terms such as "holy" or "spiritual." In choosing "generation" as the equivalent of "Geschlecht," I am relying on its biblical overtones (also present in the German term) to help focus on slight sexual connotations of its usage in King James English and in "Christian" writers such as William Blake. Nonetheless, it is obvious that its reliance on literary contexts renders it weaker than the original.

This, however, represents a rather minor instance of the difficulties encountered in translating Trakl. However difficult it may prove for an interpreter to paraphrase the significance of such choices of diction, it is relatively easy for the translator to imitate them, given the availability of English terms with ranges of signification similar to those of the German terms. There will, of course, be necessary losses, but if the translator husbands his resources well, there may also be a few compensatory gains. In regard to our final examples, however, the situation is different. These rely on a syntactical flexibility inherent in the German language, which is foreign to the genius of English.

The most elementary examples of this are provided by Trakl's use of neologism. Such usage may represent a strategy to countervail the effects of archaism. That his poems should not simply succumb to an "elevated" ambience, Trakl intersperses words with an opposing tendency, such as "Unrat" (filth) and "Verwesung" (corruption). Likewise, neology opposes the reactionary tendency of his diction. For instance, in the first part of "The West" Trakl uses the phrase "Hinüberstarben Liebende." The term "hinüberstarben" is a coinage consisting of the imperfect of the verb "to die" plus a prefix denoting motion across or outward. Although I have translated the line "lovers died across," my coinage is less than satisfactory, since it fails to convey the full sense of motion expressed by Trakl's term. But its lack of force and naturalness is merely another instance of a minor difficulty.

A better example is provided by one of the most characteristic grammatical features of Trakl's style: his predilection for indefinite singular substantive neuter forms of common adjectives. In "Passion," the second line reads, "Beklagend ein Totes im Abendgarten." The resources of English do not permit an exact rendering of this line. "Ein Totes" is a phrase intermediate in signification between "ein totes Ding" (a dead thing) and "etwas Totes" (something dead). In order to capture its combination of singularity, indefiniteness, and concreteness, I have translated it as "a death," thereby permuting an object into an event. In "The West," however, I have translated the same phrase as "something dead," and in "Amen" have rendered "Verwestes" as "corruption." The problem with such solutions is that they miss the "strangeness" of Trakl's diction, by means of which he distances the reader from what is portrayed. Thus they fail to weaken the ordinary rational associations of discourse in favor of its more affective elements. But this point will become clearer through consideration of a final example.

The fourth line of "Passion" reads, "Es rauscht die Klage das herbstliche Rohr." This line, which exhibits Trakl as a master of the flexibility of German syntax, exemplifies a construction possible (though rare) in German, but impossible in English. It begins with the indefinite pronoun "es" followed by a verb, which, if it were intransitive, could be translated by the somewhat archaic English construction "there" plus a verb, as in the line "There came a knock at the door." But, since Trakl's verb is followed by two noun phrases, both of which may be in either the nominative or the accusative case, it must be transitive. The problem is to determine which of these phrases is the subject and which the object of the verb. That is, it must be decided whether the primary meaning of the line is best captured by something like "the lament rustles the autumn reed" or by something like "the autumn reed rustles the lament." The choice is not easy, for either would fit the context of the poem; however, it would seem that the initial "es" serves to signal an inversion, in which case the latter would be preferred. Nonetheless, the obvious reason why Trakl has chosen such a construction is that both meanings are intended simultaneously. This is, indeed, the main point of the line, which concerns the lamentation of Orpheus. This simultaneously *acts* on nature (as Rilke says, moving rocks and lions and trees) and *is* nature. The song vibrates the reeds; the reeds' vibration is the song. But the economy with which Trakl achieves this effect is both "super-logical" (since logic tends habitually to seek a single, "linear" meaning) and totally beyond the resources of English (whose reliance on word order rather than inflection makes a single meaning obligatory). Whereas in German the ambiguity of the line is a major aspect of its beauty and its very *raison d'être*, the translator is compelled both to mangle that beauty and to destroy that *raison*, turning a refusal of our habit of causal thinking into one more reinforcement of that habit. Whereas the German reader is invited to feel his way through the beauty of the line into the marriage of both senses, the English reader is left with half a text and a fragment of its sense.

The translator must attempt to compensate for such losses by whatever means he commands, holding, in the process, as closely to the spirit of the original as he can. This, at least, has been my aim, and the present selection represents those poems of Trakl for which I have found the richest and most faithful compensations. Happily, it also contains most of the poems for which he is famous, and thus may lay claim to being an introduction to his work.

In all cases the text is that established by Walther Killy in his critical edition.[22] I have, however, taken the liberty of dividing the poems into two sections. The first consists of eight rhymed poems, which are meant primarily as a sample of Trakl's work within this format. Since the contrast between "form and content" is a major aspect of such poems, I have considered their rhyme indispensable, and have translated accordingly. This has necessitated treating their "content" somewhat loosely, and thus I have separated them from those of the second section, which make up the bulk of this volume. With these, which are unrhymed, I have been able to follow my standards of fidelity in a manner more to my satisfaction. I have tried, that is, to say as well as possible in English what Trakl has said in German. If my versions serve somehow to "infect" the reader with the "truth" of Trakl's vision, then they will have achieved their purpose.

Notes to the Introduction

1. Walther Killy, *Über Georg Trakl*, 3rd ed. (Gottingen: Vandenhoek und Ruprecht Verlag, 1967), 3.
2. Quoted in Erich Neumann, "Georg Trakl: The Person and the Myth," in *Creative Man* (Princeton: Princeton University Press, 1979), 146.
3. Theodor Spoerri, *Georg Trakl: Strukturen in Persönlichkeit und Werk* (Bern: Francke Verlag, 1954), 41.
4. Quoted in Killy, *Trakl*, 85. My translation.

4. Quoted in Killy, *Trakl*, 85. My translation.

5. *Ibid.*, 52. My translation.

6. *Ibid.*, 88. My translation.

7. Quoted in Herbert Lindenberger, *Georg Trakl* (New York: Twayne Publishers, Inc., 1971), 31.

8. Quoted in Johannes Klein, "Georg Trakl," in *Expressionismus als Literatur*, Rothe, ed. (Bern: Francke Verlag, 1969), 388. My translation.

9. *Ibid.*, 381. My translation.

10. Quoted in Lindenberger, *Trakl*, 26.

11. Quoted in Kurt Pinthus, *Menschheitsdämmerung* (Hamburg: Rowohlt Verlag, 1959), 363. My translation.

12. Quoted in Lindenberger, *Trakl*.

13. Quoted in Klein, "Trakl," 384. My translation.

14. Quoted in Killy, *Trakl*, 52. My translation.

15. Walter H. Sokel, *The Writer in Extremis* (Stanford: Stanford University Press, 1959), 49ff.

16. Francis Michael Sharp, *The Poet's Madness: A Reading of Georg Trakl* (Ithaca: Cornell University Press, 1981), 46f.

17. Quoted in Killy, *Trakl*, 5. My translation.

18. R. M. Rilke, *Briefe* (Wiesbaden: Insel Verlag, 1950), 527. My translation.

19. Killy, *Trakl*, 86. My translation.

20. *Ibid.*, 92f. My translation.

21. *Ibid.*, 89f. My translation.

22. Georg Trakl, *Dichtungen und Briefe* (Salzburg: Otto Müller Verlag, 1969).

SONG *of the* WEST

I

Traum des Bösen

Verhallend eines Gongs braungoldne Klänge—
Ein Liebender erwacht in schwarzen Zimmern
Die Wang' an Flammen, die im Fenster flimmern.
Am Strome blitzen Segel, Masten, Stränge.

Ein Mönch, ein schwangres Weib dort im Gedränge
Guitarren klimpern, rote Kittel schimmern.
Kastanien schwül in goldnem Glanz verkümmern;
Schwarz ragt der Kirchen trauriges Gepränge.

Aus bleichen Masken schaut der Geist des Bösen.
Ein Platz verdämmert grauenvoll und düster;
Am Abend regt auf Inseln sich Geflüster.

Des Vogelfluges wirre Zeichen lesen
Aussätzige, die zur Nacht vielleicht verwesen.
Im Park erblicken zitternd sich Geschwister.

Dream of Evil

A gong's brown-golden tones no longer loud—
A lover wakes in chambers growing dimmer,
His cheek near flames that in the window glimmer.
Upon the stream flash rigging, mast and shroud.

A monk, a pregnant woman in the crowd;
Guitars are strumming, scarlet dresses shimmer.
In golden gleam the chestnuts shrink and simmer;
The churches' mournful pomp looms black and proud.

The evil spirit peers from masks of white.
A square grows gloomy, hideous and stark;
Whispers arise on islands in the dark.

Lepers, who rot away perhaps at night,
Read convoluted omens of birdflight.
Siblings eye each other, trembling in the park.

Ein Winterabend

Wenn der Schnee ans Fenster fällt,
Lang die Abendglocke läutet,
Vielen ist der Tisch bereitet
Und das Haus ist wohlbestellt.

Mancher auf der Wanderschaft
Kommt ans Tor auf dunklen Pfaden.
Golden blüht der Baum der Gnaden
Aus der Erde kühlem Saft.

Wanderer tritt still herein;
Schmerz versteinerte die Schwelle.
Da erglänzt in reiner Helle
Auf dem Tische Brot und Wein.

A Winter Evening

When snow falls at the windowside,
Long the evening bell shall toll;
For many is the table full,
And the house is well-supplied.

Some have come in journey's dearth
To the gate from darkened ways.
Golden blooms the tree of grace
From the cool sap of the earth.

Wanderer, come in and dine;
Pain has petrified the sill.
In pure splendor sparkle still
On the table bread and wine.

Entlang

Geschnitten sind Korn und Traube,
Der Weiler in Herbst und Ruh.
Hammer und Amboß klingt immerzu,
Lachen in purpurner Laube.

Astern von dunklen Zäunen
Bring dem weißen Kind.
Sag wie lang wir gestorben sind;
Sonne will schwarz erscheinen.

Rotes Fischlein im Weiher;
Stirn, die sich fürchtig belauscht;
Abendwind leise ans Fenster rauscht,
Blaues Orgelgeleier.

Stern und heimlich Gefunkel
Läßt noch einmal aufschaun.
Erscheinung der Mutter in Schmerz und Graun;
Schwarze Reseden im Dunkel.

Along

Cut are the grapes and the sheaves,
The hamlet in autumn and peace.
Hammer and anvil clang without cease,
Laughter in the crimson leaves.

To the white child bring back
Asters from the dark bed.
Tell us how long we have been dead;
The sun will appear black.

Little red fish in the pond;
Brow that lurks listening in fright.
Evening wind rattles the windows so light,
Organ's blue tremulous sound.

Star and mysterious spark
Draw the gaze upward again.
The mother appears in horror and pain;
Black mignonettes in the dark.

Herbstseele

Jägerruf und Blutgebell;
Hinter Kreuz und braunem Hügel
Blindet sacht der Weiherspiegel,
Schreit der Habicht hart und hell.

Über Stoppelfeld und Pfad
Banget schon ein schwarzes Schweigen;
Reiner Himmel in den Zweigen;
Nur der Bach rinnt still und stad.

Bald entgleitet Fisch und Wild.
Blaue Seele, dunkles Wandern
Schied uns bald von Lieben, Andern.
Abend wechselt Sinn und Bild.

Rechten Lebens Brot und Wein,
Gott in deine milden Hände
Legt der Mensch das dunkle Ende,
Alle Schuld und rote Pein.

Soul of Autumn

Cry of hunter, bay of hound;
Beyond the cross and the brown hill
The hawk is shrieking hard and shrill;
Soft is the dazzle of the pond.

Above the path and stubblefield
Black silence already cowers;
Purest heaven in the bowers;
The brook alone flows calm and mild.

Fish and prey soon flee our glance.
Blue soul, the dark where we go
Parts us soon from friend and foe.
Evening shuffles sight and sense.

Bread and wine of righteous life,
God, into your gentle hands
Man will lay his lightless end,
All his guilt and crimson strife.

Afra

Ein Kind mit braunem Haar. Gebet und Amen
Verdunkeln still die abendliche Kühle
Und Afras Lächeln rot in gelbem Rahmen
Von Sonnenblumen, Angst und grauer Schwüle.

Gehüllt in blauen Mantel sah vor Zeiten
Der Mönch sie fromm gemalt an Kirchenfenstern;
Das will in Schmerzen freundlich noch geleiten,
Wenn ihre Sterne durch sein Blut gespenstern.

Herbstuntergang; und des Holunders Schweigen.
Die Stirne rührt des Wassers blaue Regung,
Ein härnes Tuch gelegt auf eine Bahre.

Verfaulte Früchte fallen von den Zweigen;
Unsäglich ist der Vögel Flug, Begegnung
Mit Sterbenden; dem folgen dunkle Jahre.

Afra

A child with brown hair. Prayer and holy name
Darken with calm the coolness of the night,
And Afra's smile, red in a yellow frame
Of sunflowers, gray sultriness and fright.

Wrapped in a blue cloak, the monk in times past
Saw her on church windows devoutly painted;
Even in pain such fellowship will last,
When, traversed by her stars, his blood is haunted.

Autumn declines; the elderbush grows mute.
The brow brushes the water's blue waves beating,
A cloth of hair folded upon a bier.

Out of the branches fall the rotten fruit.
Unspeakable the flight of birds, a meeting
With the dying; dark year follows year.

Der Herbst des Einsamen

Der dunkle Herbst kehrt ein voll Frucht und Fülle,
Vergilbter Glanz von schönen Sommertagen.
Ein reines Blau tritt aus verfallener Hülle;
Der Flug der Vögel tönt von alten Sagen.
Gekeltert ist der Wein, die milde Stille
Erfüllt von leiser Antwort dunkler Fragen.

Und hier und dort ein Kreuz auf ödem Hügel;
Im roten Wald verliert sich eine Herde.
Die Wolke wandert übern Weiherspiegel;
Es ruht des Landmanns ruhige Geberde.
Sehr leise rührt des Abends blauer Flügel
Ein Dach von dürrem Stroh, die schwarze Erde.

Bald nisten Sterne in des Müden Brauen;
In kühle Stuben kehrt ein still Bescheiden
Und Engel treten leise aus den blauen
Augen der Liebenden, die sanfter leiden.
Es rauscht das Rohr; anfällt ein knöchern Grauen,
Wenn schwarz der Tau tropft von den kahlen Weiden.

The Autumn of the Lonely One

The dark autumn enters with fruit and fullness,
The yellowed sheen of lovely summer days.
A pure blue flows from husks of moldered dullness;
The flight of birds resounds with ancient lays.
The wine is trodden out; the mild stillness
Resolves dark questions with its soft replies.

And here and there a cross on a bleak hill;
In the red woods a flock has wandered forth.
Clouds roam across the surface of the pool;
Peaceful the mien of him of rural birth.
The evening's blue wing brushes, very still,
A roof of brittle straw and the black earth.

Soon stars will nest within the tired one's gaze;
Into cool rooms silent content will follow;
And angels softly step from the blue eyes
Of lovers, whose torments have grown more mellow.
The reed is rustling; bony shivers rise
When the black dew drops from the naked willow.

Klage

Jüngling aus kristallnem Munde
Sank dein goldner Blick ins Tal;
Waldes Woge rot und fahl
In der schwarzen Abendstunde.
Abend schlägt so tiefe Wunde!

Angst! des Todes Traumbeschwerde,
Abgestorben Grab und gar
Schaut aus Baum und Wild das Jahr;
Kahles Feld und Ackererde.
Ruft der Hirt die bange Herde.

Schwester, deine blauen Brauen
Winken leise in der Nacht.
Orgel seufzt und Hölle lacht
Und es faßt das Herz ein Grauen;
Möchte Stern und Engel schauen.

Mutter muß ums Kindlein zagen;
Rot ertönt im Schacht das Erz,
Wollust, Tränen, steinern Schmerz,
Der Titanen dunkle Sagen.
Schwermut! einsam Adler klagen.

Plaint

From the crystal mouth, youth, seep
Your gold glances in the vale;
The forest's surge is red and pale
In the black hour before sleep.
Evening inflicts wounds so deep.

Fear! the dream-complaints of death,
Withered grave, and worse, the year
Gazes out of tree and deer;
Naked field and planted earth.
The shepherd calls his cowed flock forth.

Sister, your eyebrows of blue
Beckon softly in the night.
Organs sigh and hell laughs bright,
And the heart is seized with rue;
I will see stars and angels too.

For her child mother must quake;
The ore rings crimson in the vein,
Lust and tears and stony pain;
Titan legends ever bleak.
Despair! alone, the eagles shriek.

Nachtergebung

Mönchin! schließ mich in dein Dunkel,
Ihr Gebirge kühl und blau!
Niederblutet dunkler Tau;
Kreuz ragt steil im Sterngefunkel.

Purpurn brachen Mund und Lüge
In verfallner Kammer kühl;
Scheint noch Lachen, golden Spiel,
Einer Glocke letzte Züge.

Mondeswolke! Schwärzlich fallen
Wilde Früchte nachts vom Baum
Und zum Grabe wird der Raum
Und zum Traum dies Erdenwallen.

Night Surrender

Monk-girl, close me in your dark;
O you mountains, cool and blue!
Downward bleeds the darkened dew;
In starlight the cross looms stark.

Crimson broke both mouth and lies
In the ruined chambers' cold;
Laughter comes with games of gold,
And the bells' last echo dies.

Mooncloud! wild fruits at night's seam
From the tree fall in the gloom;
And all space becomes a tomb,
The seething of the earth a dream.

II

De profundis

Es ist ein Stoppelfeld, in das ein schwarzer Regen fällt.
Es ist ein brauner Baum, der einsam dasteht.
Es ist ein Zischelwind, der leere Hütten umkreist.
Wie traurig dieser Abend.

Am Weiler vorbei
Sammelt die sanfte Waise noch spärliche Ähren ein.
Ihre Augen weiden rund und goldig in der Dämmerung
Und ihr Schoß harrt des himmlischen Bräutigams.

Bei der Heimkehr
Fanden die Hirten den süßen Leib
Verwest im Dornenbusch.

Ein Schatten bin ich ferne finsteren Dörfern.
Gottes Schweigen
Trank ich aus dem Brunnen des Hains.

Auf meine Stirne tritt kaltes Metall
Spinnen suchen mein Herz.
Est ist ein Licht, das in meinem Mund erlöscht.

Nachts fand ich mich auf einer Heide,
Starrend von Unrat und Staub der Sterne.
Im Haselgebüsch
Klangen wieder kristallne Engel.

De Profundis

It is a stubblefield, in which a black rain falls.
It is a brown tree, which stands there alone.
It is a hissing wind, which circles empty huts.
How sorrowful this evening.

Beyond the hamlet
Still the gentle orphan gleans her scanty grain.
Her eyes feed wide and golden in the twilight
And her womb trusts in the heavenly bridegroom.

Returning home,
The shepherds found the sweet corpse
Rotting in a thornbush.

I am a shadow far from darkened villages.
I drank
God's silence from the fountain in the grove.

Cold metal stands upon my brow;
Spiders seek my heart.
It is a light, which goes out in my mouth.

At night I found myself upon a heath,
Stiff with filth and stardust.
In the hazelbush
Crystal angels rang again.

Amen

Verwestes gleitend durch die morsche Stube;
Schatten an gelben Tapeten; in dunklen Spiegeln wölbt
Sich unserer Hände elfenbeinerne Traurigkeit.

Braune Perlen rinnen durch die erstorbenen Finger.
In der Stille
Tun sich eines Engels blaue Mohnaugen auf.

Blau ist auch der Abend;
Die Stunde unseres Absterbens, Azraels Schatten,
Der ein braunes Gärtchen verdunkelt.

Amen

Corruption drifting through the musty room,
Shadows on yellow tapestries; the ivory sorrow
Of our hands arches in dark mirrors.

Brown pearls run through stiffened fingers.
An angel's
Poppy-eyes of blue open in the silence.

Blue also is the evening;
The hour of our dying, Azrael's shadow,
Which darkens a brown garden.

Abendlied

Am Abend, wenn wir auf dunklen Pfaden gehn,
Erscheinen unsere bleichen Gestalten vor uns.

Wenn uns dürstet,
Trinken wir die weißen Wasser des Teichs,
Die Süße unserer traurigen Kindheit.

Erstorbene ruhen wir unterm Holundergebüsch,
Schaun den grauen Möven zu.

Frühlingsgewölke steigen über die finstere Stadt,
Die der Mönche edlere Zeiten schweigt.

Da ich deine schmalen Hände nahm
Schlugst du leise die runden Augen auf,
Dieses ist lange her.

Doch wenn dunkler Wohllaut die Seele heimsucht,
Erscheinst du Weiße in des Freundes herbstlicher Landschaft.

Evening Song

At evening, when we walk upon dark paths,
Our pallid forms appear before us.

When we are thirsty,
We drink the white water of the pond,
The sweetness of our sorrowful childhood.

Benumbed, we rest beneath the elderbush;
We watch the gray seagull.

Springtime clouds rise above the black city,
Which does not speak the nobler seasons of the monks.

As I took your slender hands,
Softly you opened your wide eyes;
That was long ago.

But when dark sonority haunts the soul,
White, you appear in your friend's autumnal landscape.

Nachtlied

Des Unbewegten Odem. Ein Tiergesicht
Erstarrt vor Bläue, ihrer Heiligkeit.
Gewaltig ist das Schweigen im Stein;

Die Maske eines nächtlichen Vogels. Sanfter Dreiklang
Verklingt in einem. Elai! dein Antlitz
Beugt sich sprachlos über bläuliche Wasser.

O! ihr stillen Spiegel der Wahrheit.
An des Einsamen elfenbeinerner Schläfe
Erscheint der Abglanz gefallener Engel.

Night Song

The breath of the Unmoved. An animal face
Grows stiff with blue, with its holiness.
Mighty is the stillness in the stone,

The mask of a nightbird. A gentle triad
Ebbs into unity. Elai! your countenance
Bows speechlessly above the bluish water.

O you silent mirrors of truth!
On the ivory temples of the lonely one
Appears the reflection of fallen angels.

Helian

In den einsamen Stunden des Geistes
Ist es schön, in der Sonne zu gehn
An den gelben Mauern des Sommers hin.
Leise klingen die Schritte im Gras; doch immer schläft
Der Sohn des Pan im grauen Marmor.

Abends auf der Terrasse betranken wir uns mit braunem Wein.
Rötlich glüht der Pfirsich im Laub;
Sanfte Sonate, frohes Lachen.

Schön ist die Stille der Nacht.
Auf dunklem Plan
Begegnen wir uns mit Hirten und weißen Sternen.

Wenn es Herbst geworden ist
Zeigt sich nüchterne Klarheit im Hain.
Besänftigte wandeln wir an roten Mauern hin
Und die runden Augen folgen dem Flug der Vögel.
Am Abend sinkt das weiße Wasser in Graburnen.

In kahlen Gezweigen feiert der Himmel.
In reinen Händen trägt der Landmann Brot und Wein
Und friedlich reifen die Früchte in sonniger Kammer.

O wie ernst ist das Antlitz der teueren Toten.
Doch die Seele erfreut gerechtes Anschaun.

Helian

In the solitary hours of the spirit
It is beautiful to walk in the sun
Along the yellow walls of summer.
Faintly our footsteps ring in the grass; yet always
The son of Pan sleeps in the gray marble.

At evening on the terrace we got drunk with brown wine.
The peach glows red within the foliage;
Gentle sonata, merry laughter.

Beautiful is the silence of the night.
On the dark plain
We meet with shepherds and white stars.

When autumn comes,
A sober clarity enters the grove.
Appeased, we wander along the red walls
And our wide eyes follow the flight of birds.
At evening white water sinks in the urns.

Heaven rejoices in the naked branches.
In his pure hands the countryman bears bread and wine
And fruit ripens peacefully in the sunny chamber.

Oh how solemn is the countenance of the precious dead.
Yet righteous regard delights the soul.

Gewaltig ist das Schweigen des verwüsteten Gartens,
Da der junge Novize die Stirne mit braunem Laub bekränzt,
Sein Odem eisiges Gold trinkt.

Die Hände rühren das Alter bläulicher Wasser
Oder in kalter Nacht die weißen Wangen der Schwestern.

Leise und harmonisch ist ein Gang an freundlichen Zimmern hin,
Wo Einsamkeit ist und das Rauschen des Ahorns,
Wo vielleicht noch die Drossel singt.

Schön ist der Mensch und erscheinend im Dunkel,
Wenn er staunend Arme und Beine bewegt,
Und in purpurnen Höhlen stille die Augen rollen.

Zur Vesper verliert sich der Fremdling in schwarzer
        Novemberzerstörung,
Unter morschem Geäst, an Mauern voll Aussatz hin,
Wo vordem der heilige Bruder gegangen,
Versunken in das sanfte Saitenspiel seines Wahnsinns,

O wie einsam endet der Abendwind.
Ersterbend neigt sich das Haupt im Dunkel des Ölbaums.

Mighty is the silence of the ravaged garden.
As the young novice wreathes his brow with brown foliage,
His breath drinks icy gold.

His hands touch the age of the bluish water
Or the white cheeks of the sisters in the cold night.

Soft and harmonious is a walk along cheerful chambers,
Where there is solitude and the rustling of a maple,
Where the thrush perhaps still sings.

Beautiful is man, and appearing in darkness,
When astonished he moves his arms and legs
And his eyes roll silently in their crimson sockets.

The stranger vanishes at Vesper in the black destruction of November,
Beneath moldy branches, along walls full of leprosy,
Where the holy brother has gone before,
Immersed in the gentle string music of his madness,

Oh how lonely ceases the evening wind.
Dying, his head bows down in the darkness of the olive tree.

Erschütternd ist der Untergang des Geschlechts.
In dieser Stunde füllen sich die Augen des Schauenden
Mit dem Gold seine Sterne.

Am Abend versinkt ein Glockenspiel, das nicht mehr tönt,
Verfallen die schwarzen Mauern am Platz,
Ruft der tote Soldat zum Gebet.

Ein bleicher Engel
Tritt der Sohn ins leere Haus seiner Väter.

Die Schwestern sind ferne zu weißen Greisen gegangen.
Nachts fand sie der Schläfer unter den Säulen im Hausflur,
Zurückgekehrt von traurigen Pilgerschaften.

O wie starrt von Kot und Würmern ihr Haar,
Da er darein mit silbernen Füßen steht,
Und jene verstorben aus kahlen Zimmern treten.

O ihr Psalmen in feurigen Mitternachtsregen,
Da die Knechte mit Nesseln die sanften Augen schlugen,
Die kindlichen Früchte des Holunders
Sich staunend neigen über ein leeres Grab.

Leise rollen vergilbte Monde
Über die Fieberlinnen des Jünglings,
Eh dem Schweigen des Winters folgt.

Shattering is the oblivion of the flesh.
In this hour the eyes of the watcher
Fill with the gold of his stars.

A glockenspiel ebbs at evening, and rings no longer,
On the square the black walls crumble,
The dead soldier calls to prayer.

A pallid angel,
The son steps into the empty house of his fathers.

The sisters have journeyed afar to the white elders.
At night the sleeper found them under pillars in the hallway,
Returned from sorrowful pilgrimage.

Oh how stiff is their hair with filth and worms,
As he stands in it with silver feet,
And dead they step from the naked chambers.

O you psalms in fiery midnight rains,
As the servants smote the gentle eyes with nettles,
The childlike fruits of the elderbush
Bend astonished above an empty grave.

Yellowed moons roll softly
Above the fever linen of the youth
Before the silence of winter comes.

Ein erhabenes Schicksal sinnt den Kidron hinab,
Wo die Zeder, ein weiches Geschöpf,
Sich unter den blauen Brauen des Vaters entfaltet,
Über die Weide nachts ein Schäfer seine Herde führt.
Oder es sind Schreie im Schlaf,
Wenn ein eherner Engel im Hain den Menschen antritt,
Das Fleisch des Heiligen auf glühendem Rost hinschmilzt.

Um die Lehmhütten rankt purpurner Wein,
Tönende Bündel vergilbten Korns,
Das Summen der Bienen, der Flug des Kranichs.
Am Abend begegnen sich Auferstandene auf Felsenpfaden.

In schwarzen Wassern spiegeln sich Aussätzige;
Oder sie öffnen die kotbeileckten Gewänder
Weinend dem balsamischen Wind, der vom rosigen Hügel weht.

Schlanke Mägde tasten durch die Gassen der Nacht,
Ob sie den liebenden Hirten fänden.
Sonnabends tönt in den Hütten sanfter Gesang.

Lasset das Lied auch des Knaben gedenken,
Seines Wahnsinns, und weißer Brauen und seines Hingangs,
Des Verwesten, der bläulich die Augen aufschlägt.
O wie traurig ist dieses Wiedersehn.

A superior fate muses down the Kidron,
Where the cedar, a gentle creature,
Unfolds beneath the blue eyebrows of the father,
A shepherd leads his flock across the pasture by night.
Or there are cries in sleep,
When a brazen angel encounters the man in the grove,
The flesh of the saint melts away on the glowing grate.

About clay huts twine purple grapes,
Ringing sheaves of yellowed corn,
The humming of bees, the flight of the crane.
On rocky paths the resurrected gather in the evening.

In the black waters lepers are mirrored;
Or they open their filth-besplattered garments,
Weeping to the wind of balsam, wafting from the rosy hill.

Through the alleys slender maidens grope at night,
Seeking the loving shepherds.
On Saturdays gentle choruses ring in the huts.

May the song also remember the boy,
His madness, his white eyebrows and his departure,
The corrupted, who bluishly opens his eyes.
O how sorrowful is this reencounter.

Die Stufen des Wahnsinns in schwarzen Zimmern,
Die Schatten der Alten unter der offenen Tür,
Da Helians Seele sich im rosigen Spiegel beschaut
Und Schnee und Aussatz von seiner Stirne sinken.

An den Wänden sind die Sterne erloschen
Und die weißen Gestalten des Lichts.

Dem Teppich entsteigt Gebein der Gräber,
Das Schweigen verfallener Kreuze am Hügel,
Des Weihrauchs Süße im purpurnen Nachtwind.

O ihr zerbrochenen Augen in schwarzen Mündern,
Da der Enkel in sanfter Umnachtung
Einsam dem dunkleren Ende nachsinnt,
Der stille Gott die blauen Lider über ihn senkt.

The steps of madness in black chambers,
The shadows of the aged beneath the open door,
When Helian's soul beholds itself in the rosy mirror,
And snow and leprosy drop from his brow.

Along the walls the stars are extinguished,
And the white shapes of light.

The bones of the graves rise up from the carpet,
The silence of the broken crosses on the hill,
The sweetness of incense in the crimson nightwind.

O you shattered eyes in black mouths,
As the grandchild alone in gentle derangement
Contemplates the darker end,
Above him the silent god lowers his blue eyelids.

Landschaft

Septemberabend; traurig tönen die dunklen Rufe der Hirten
Durch das dämmernde Dorf; Feuer sprüht in der Schmiede.
Gewaltig bäumt sich ein schwarzes Pferd; die hyazinthenen
    Locken der Magd
Haschen nach der Inbrunst seiner purpurnen Nüstern.
Leise erstarrt am Saum des Waldes der Schrei der Hirschkuh
Und die gelben Blumen des Herbstes
Neigen sich sprachlos über das blaue Antlitz des Teichs.
In roter Flamme verbrannte ein Baum; aufflattern mit dunklen
    Gesichtern die Fledermäuse.

Landscape

September evening: mournfully the dark cries of the shepherds
Ring through the dusky village; fire spits in the forge.
A black horse rears up violently; the girl's hyacinthine locks
Snatch at the ardor of its crimson nostrils.
Softly the cry of the doe freezes at the edge of the forest
And the yellow blossoms of autumn
Bend speechlessly above the blue countenance of the pond.
In red flames a tree burned down; bats flap upward with dark faces.

An den Knaben Elis

Elis, wenn die Amsel im schwarzen Wald ruft,
Dieses ist dein Untergang.
Deine Lippen trinken die Kühle des blauen Felsenquells.

Laß, wenn deine Stirne leise blutet
Uralte Legenden
Und dunkle Deutung des Vogelflugs.

Du aber gehst mit weichen Schritten in die Nacht,
Die voll purpurner Trauben hängt,
Und du regst die Arme schöner im Blau.

Ein Dornenbusch tönt,
Wo deine mondenen Augen sind.
O, wie lange bist, Elis, du verstorben.

Dein Leib ist eine Hyazinthe,
In die ein Mönch die wächsernen Finger taucht.
Eine schwarze Höhle ist unser Schweigen,

Daraus bisweilen ein sanftes Tier tritt
Und langsam die schweren Lider senkt.
Auf deine Schläfen tropft schwarzer Tau,

Das letzte Gold verfallener Sterne.

To the Child Elis

Elis, when the blackbird calls in the black forest,
This is your oblivion.
Your lips drink the cool of the blue rockspring.

Let go, when your brow softly bleeds
Ancient legends
And dark readings of birdflight.

But you pass with soft footsteps into the night
Which is hanging full of purple grapes,
And you move your arms more beautifully in the blue.

A thornbush sings
Where your moonlit eyes are.
Oh how long, Elis, have you been dead!

Your body is a hyacinth,
Into which a monk dips his waxen fingers.
A black cavern is our silence,

From which at times a gentle beast steps
And slowly lowers its heavy eyelids.
Upon your temples drops black dew,

The final gold of fallen stars.

Elis

1

Vollkommen ist die Stille dieses goldenen Tags.
Unter alten Eichen
Erscheinst du, Elis, ein Ruhender mit runden Augen.

Ihre Bläue spiegelt den Schlummer der Liebenden.
An deinem Mund
Verstummten ihre rosigen Seufzer.

Am Abend zog der Fischer die schweren Netze ein.
Ein guter Hirt
Führt seine Herde am Waldsaum hin.
O! wie gerecht sind, Elis, alle deine Tage.

Leise sinkt
An kahlen Mauern des Ölbaums blaue Stille,
Erstirbt eines Greisen dunkler Gesang.

Ein goldener Kahn
Schaukelt, Elis, dein Herz am einsamen Himmel.

Elis

1

Perfect is the silence of this golden day.
Beneath ancient oaktrees
You appear, Elis, at rest with wide eyes.

Their blue mirrors the slumber of lovers.
On your mouth
Their rosy sighs were stilled.

At evening the fisherman hauled in his heavy nets.
A good shepherd
Leads his flock along the forest's edge.
Oh how righteous, Elis, are your days!

Softly the blue silence
Of the olive tree sinks near the naked walls,
The dark song of an old man dies away.

A golden skiff,
Your heart rocks, Elis, on the lonely sky.

2

Ein sanftes Glockenspiel tönt in Elis' Brust
Am Abend,
Da sein Haupt ins schwarze Kissen sinkt.

Ein blaues Wild
Blutet leise im Dorngestrüpp.

Ein brauner Baum steht abgeschieden da;
Seine blauen Früchte fielen von ihm.

Zeichen und Sterne
Versinken leise im Abendweiher.

Hinter dem Hügel ist es Winter geworden.

Blaue Tauben
Trinken nachts den eisigen Schweiß,
Der von Elis' kristallener Stirne rinnt.

Immer tönt
An schwarzen Mauern Gottes einsamer Wind.

2

A gentle glockenspiel sings in Elis' breast
At evening,
When his head sinks into the black pillow.

A blue prey
Bleeds softly in the thornbrush.

A brown tree stands in isolation there;
Its blue fruits have fallen from it.

Signs and stars
Sink softly in the evening pond.

Beyond the hill it has turned winter.

At night
Blue doves drink up the icy sweat
That flows from Elis' crystal brow.

Along black walls
Forever drones the lonely wind of God.

Sebastian im Traum

Für Adolf Loos

1

Mutter trug das Kindlein im weißen Mond,
Im Schatten des Nußbaums, uralten Holunders,
Trunken vom Safte des Mohns, der Klage der Drossel;
Und stille
Neigte in Mitlied sich über jene ein bärtiges Antlitz

Leise im Dunkel des Fensters; und altes Hausgerät
Der Väter
Lag im Verfall; Liebe und herbstliche Träumerei.

Also dunkel der Tag des Jahrs, traurige Kindheit,
Da der Knabe leise zu kühlen Wassern, silbernen Fischen hinabstieg,
Ruh und Antlitz;
Da er steinern sich vor rasende Rappen warf,
In grauer Nacht sein Stern über ihn kam;

Oder wenn er an der frierenden Hand der Mutter
Abends über Sankt Peters herbstlichen Friedhof ging,
Ein zarter Leichnam stille im Dunkel der Kammer lag
Und jener die kalten Lider über ihn aufhob.

Er aber war ein kleiner Vogel im kahlen Geäst,
Die Glocke lang im Abendnovember,
Des Vaters Stille, da er im Schlaf die dämmernde Wendeltreppe
      hinabstieg.

Sebastian Dreaming

for Adolf Loos

1

Mother bore the little child in the white moon,
In the shadow of the nut tree, the ancient elder,
Drunk on the sap of the poppy, the plaint of the thrush,
And silently
A bearded countenance bent over her with pity,

Softly in the darkness of the window; the ancient household
Of the fathers
Lay in ruins; love and autumn reverie.

Thus dark was the day of the year, sorrowful childhood,
When the boy descended softly to cool waters, silver fishes,
Rest and countenance;
When he threw himself stonily before black raging stallions,
Then his star rose above him in the gray night;

Or if he went by evening at his mother's icy hand
Across St. Peter's autumn cemetery,
A frail corpse lay silent in the dark of his chamber
And lifted its cold lids above him.

But he was a small bird in the naked branches,
The bells long in evening November,
The father's silence, when in sleep he descended the dusky spiral stairs.

2

Frieden der Seele. Einsamer Winterabend,
Die dunklen Gestalten der Hirten am alten Weiher;
Kindlein in der Hütte von Stroh; o wie leise
Sank in schwarzem Fieber das Antlitz hin.
Heilige Nacht.

Oder wenn er an der harten Hand des Vaters
Stille den finstern Kalvarienberg hinanstieg
Und in dämmernden Felsennischen
Die blaue Gestalt des Menschen durch seine Legende ging,
Aus der Wunde unter dem Herzen purpurn das Blut rann.
O wie leise stand in dunkler Seele das Kreuz auf.

Liebe; da in schwarzen Winkeln der Schnee schmolz,
Ein blaues Lüftchen sich heiter im alten Holunder fing,
In dem Schattengewölbe des Nußbaums;
Und dem Knaben leise sein rosiger Engel erschien.

Freude; da in kühlen Zimmern eine Abendsonate erklang,
Im braunen Holzgebälk
Ein blauer Falter aus der silbernen Puppe kroch.

O die Nähe des Todes. In steinerner Mauer
Neigte sich ein gelbes Haupt, schweigend das Kind,
Da in jenem März der Mond verfiel.

2

Peace of the soul. Lonely winter evening,
The dark shapes of shepherds on the ancient pond,
The little child in the hut of straw; oh how softly
The countenance sank into black fever.
O holy night.

Or if in silence at his father's stony hand
He ascended the dark Mount of Calvary
And in the dusky rock alcoves
The blue shape of man passed through his legends,
Then the blood flowed crimson from the wound below the heart.
Oh how softly the cross rose in the dark soul.

Love: when the snow melted in black corners,
A blue breeze tangled gaily in the ancient elder,
In the shadow-vault of the nut tree;
And to the boy his rosy angel softly showed.

Joy: when an evening sonata rang in cool chambers,
And from brown wooden rafters
A blue moth crept out of its silver cocoon.

O the nearness of death. In the stone wall
A yellow head bent down, silent the child,
As in that March the moon decayed.

3

Rosige Osterglocke im Grabgewölbe der Nacht
Und die Silberstimmen der Sterne,
Daß in Schauern ein dunkler Wahnsinn von der Stirne des Schläfers
   sank.

O wie stille ein Gang den blauen Fluß hinab
Vergessenes sinnend, da im grünen Geäst
Die Drossel ein Fremdes in den Untergang rief.

Oder wenn er an der knöchernen Hand des Greisen
Abends vor die verfallene Mauer der Stadt ging
Und jener in schwarzem Mantel ein rosiges Kindlein trug,
Im Schatten des Nußbaums der Geist des Bösen erschien.

Tasten über die grünen Stufen des Sommers. O wie leise
Verfiel der Garten in der braunen Stille des Herbstes,
Duft und Schwermut des alten Holunders,
Da in Sebastians Schatten die Silberstimme des Engels erstarb.

3

Rosy Easterbell in the grave-vault of the night
And the silver voices of the stars,
That a dark madness fell shuddering from the sleeper's brow.

Oh how silent a passage down the blue river,
Musing on forgotten things, when from green boughs
The thrush called strangeness into the sunset.

Or if at the old man's bony hand,
Who bore a rosy little child in a black cloak,
He passed by evening near the city's crumbled wall,
Then the spirit of evil showed in the shadow of the nut tree.

Groping above the green steps of summer. Oh how softly
The garden decayed into the brown silence of autumn.
Fragrance and melancholy of the ancient elder,
When in Sebastian's shadow the angel's silver voice died out.

Am Moor

Wanderer im schwarzen Wind; leise flüstert das dürre Rohr
In der Stille des Moors. Am grauen Himmel
Ein Zug von wilden Vögeln folgt;
Quere über finsteren Wassern.

Aufruhr. In verfallener Hütte
Aufflattert mit schwarzen Flügeln die Fäulnis;
Verkrüppelte Birken seufzen im Wind.

Abend in verlassener Schenke. Den Heimweg umwittert
Die sanfte Schwermut grasender Herden,
Erscheinung der Nacht: Kröten tauchen aus silbernen Wassern.

On the Moor

Wanderer in the black wind; the gaunt reed whispers softly
In the silence of the moors. Against the gray sky
Soars a flight of wild birds,
Crosswise over dark waters.

Uproar. In a ruined hut
Decay flaps upward on black wings;
Stunted birches sigh in the wind.

Evening in an abandoned inn. The gentle melancholy
Of grazing herds envelopes the way home.
Apparition of the night: toads emerge from silver waters.

Abend in Lans

Wanderschaft durch dämmernden Sommer
An Bündeln vergilbten Korns vorbei. Unter getünchten Bogen,
Wo die Schwalbe aus und ein flog, tranken wir feurigen Wein.

Schön: o Schwermut und purpurnes Lachen.
Abend und die dunklen Düfte des Grüns
Kühlen mit Schauern die glühende Stirne uns.

Silberne Wasser rinnen über die Stufen des Walds,
Die Nacht und sprachlos ein vergessenes Leben.
Freund; die belaubten Stege ins Dorf.

Evening in Lans

Wanderings through the dusky summer
Past sheaves of yellowed grain. Beneath whitewashed arches
We drank fiery wine, where the swallow flew in and out.

Beautiful: o melancholy and crimson laughter.
Evening and dark fragrances of green
Cool with shudders our glowing brows.

Silver waters stream over the steps of the forest,
The night and, speechless, a forgotten life.
Friend; the leafy footbridges into the village.

Kaspar Hauser Lied

Für Bessie Loos

Er wahrlich liebte die Sonne, die purpurn den Hügel hinabstieg,
Die Wege des Walds, den singenden Schwarzvogel
Und die Freude des Grüns.

Ernsthaft war sein Wohnen im Schatten des Baums
Und rein sein Antlitz.
Gott sprach eine sanfte Flamme zu seinem Herzen:
O Mensch!

Stille fand sein Schritt die Stadt am Abend;
Die dunkle Klage seines Munds:
Ich will ein Reiter werden.

Ihm aber folgte Busch und Tier,
Haus und Dämmergarten weißer Menschen
Und sein Mörder suchte nach ihm.

Frühling und Sommer und schön der Herbst
Des Gerechten, sein leiser Schritt
An den dunklen Zimmern Träumender hin.
Nachts blieb er mit seinem Stern allein;

Sah, daß Schnee fiel in kahles Gezweig
Und im dämmernden Hausflur den Schatten des Mörders.

Silbern sank des Ungebornen Haupt hin.

Kaspar Hauser Song

for Bessie Loos

He truly loved the sun, which, crimson, descended the hill,
The paths of the forest, the singing blackbird
And the joy of green.

Solemn was his dwelling in the shadow of the tree
And pure his countenance.
God spoke a gentle flame into his heart:
O man!

His footstep found the city silent in the evening;
The dark plaint of his mouth:
I want to be a horseman.

Yet bush and beast pursued him,
House and twilit garden of white people,
And his killer sought him.

Spring and summer and beautiful the autumn
Of the righteous, his light footstep
Along the dark chambers of dreamers.
At night he remained alone with his star,

Saw, that snow fell into naked branches,
And in the dusky hallway the shadow of the killer.

Silver, the head of the unborn sank down.

Nachts

Die Bläue meiner Augen ist erloschen in dieser Nacht,
Das rote Gold meines Herzens. O! wie stille brannte das Licht.
Dein blauer Mantel umfing den Sinkenden;
Dein roter Mund besiegelte des Freundes Umnachtung.

At Night

The blue of my eyes is extinguished in this night,
The red gold of my heart. Oh how still the light burned!
Your blue cloak caught about the one who sank,
Your red mouth sealed the derangement of your friend.

Ruh und Schweigen

Hirten begruben die Sonne im kahlen Wald.
Ein Fischer zog
In härenem Netz den Mond aus frierendem Weiher.

In blauem Kristall
Wohnt der bleiche Mensch, die Wang' an seine Sterne gelehnt;
Oder er neigt das Haupt in purpurnem Schlaf.

Doch immer rührt der schwarze Flug der Vögel
Den Schauenden, das Heilige blauer Blumen,
Denkt die nahe Stille Vergessenes, erloschene Engel.

Wieder nachtet die Stirne in mondenem Gestein;
Ein strahlender Jüngling
Erscheint die Schwester in Herbst und schwarzer Verwesung.

Rest and Silence

Shepherds buried the sun in the naked forest.
With a net of hair
A fisherman hauled the moon from the icy pond.

The pale man dwells
In a blue crystal, his cheek at rest against his stars,
Or he bows his head in crimson sleep.

But the black flight of birds always touches
The watcher, the holiness of blue flowers;
The nearby silence thinks forgotten things, extinguished angels.

Again the brow turns night in moonlit stone;
A radiant youth,
The sister appears in autumn and black corruption.

Anif

Erinnerung: Möven, gleitend über den dunklen Himmel
Männlicher Schwermut.
Stille wohnst du im Schatten der herbstlichen Esche,
Versunken in des Hügels gerechtes Maß;

Immer gehst du den grünen Fluß hinab,
Wenn es Abend geworden,
Tönende Liebe; friedlich begegnet das dunkle Wild,

Ein rosiger Mensch. Trunken von bläulicher Witterung
Rührt die Stirne das sterbende Laub
Und denkt das ernste Antlitz der Mutter;
O, wie alles ins Dunkel hinsinkt;

Die gestrengen Zimmer und das alte Gerät
Der Väter.
Dieses erschüttert die Brust des Fremdlings.
O, ihr Zeichen und Sterne.

Groß ist die Schuld des Geborenen. Weh, ihr goldenen Schauer
Des Todes,
Da die Seele kühlere Blüten träumt.

Immer schreit im kahlen Gezweig der nächtliche Vogel
Über des Mondenen Schritt,
Tönt ein eisiger Wind an den Mauern des Dorfs.

Anif

Remembrance: seagulls gliding across the dark heaven
Of masculine melancholy.
Silently you dwell in the shadow of the autumn ashtree,
Immersed in the righteous measure of the hill;

Always you pass down the green river
When evening has come;
Resonant love; peacefully dark prey are seen,

A rosy man. Drunk with a bluish scent,
The brow brushes the dying foliage
And thinks the solemn countenance of the mother;
Oh how everything sinks into darkness;

The ordered chambers and the ancient household
Of the fathers.
This convulses the breast of the stranger.
O you signs and stars.

Great is the guilt of the born. Woe, you golden shudders
Of death,
When the soul dreams cooler blossoms.

Always the nightbird cries in the naked branches
Above the footsteps of the moonlit one;
An icy wind resounds along the village walls.

Geburt

Gebirge: Schwärze, Schweigen und Schnee.
Rot vom Wald niedersteigt die Jagd;
O, die moosigen Blicke des Wilds.

Stille der Mutter; unter schwarzen Tannen
Öffnen sich die schlafenden Hände,
Wenn verfallen der kalte Mond erscheint.

O, die Geburt des Menschen. Nächtlich rauscht
Blaues Wasser im Felsengrund;
Seufzend erblickt sein Bild der gefallene Engel,

Erwacht ein Bleiches in dumpfer Stube.
Zwei Monde
Erglänzen die Augen der steinernen Greisin.

Weh, der Gebärenden Schrei. Mit schwarzem Flügel
Rührt die Knabenschläfe die Nacht,
Schnee, der leise aus purpurner Wolke sinkt.

Birth

Mountainland: blackness, silence and snow.
The hunt trails ruddy from the forest;
O the mossy glances of the prey.

The stillness of the mother: beneath black firs
The sleeping hands unclasp themselves,
When in decay the cold moon rises.

O the birth of man. At night
Blue water rushes down the rock abyss;
The fallen angel sees his image, sighing;

A pallid shape wakes in the musty room.
Two moons
Light in the eyes of the stone crone.

Woe, the cry of birthgiving. With black wings
The night brushes the boyish temples,
Snow, sinking light from purple clouds.

Untergang

An Karl Borromaeus Heinrich

Über den weißen Weiher
Sind die wilden Vögel fortgezogen.
Am Abend weht von unseren Sternen ein eisiger Wind.

Über unsere Gräber
Beugt sich die zerbrochene Stirne der Nacht.
Unter Eichen schaukeln wir auf einem silbernen Kahn.

Immer klingen die weißen Mauern der Stadt.
Unter Dornenbogen
O mein Bruder klimmen wir blinde Zeiger gen Mitternacht.

Decline

to Karl Borromaeus Heinrich

Above the white pond
The wild birds have flown away.
An icy wind blows from our stars at evening.

Above our graves
The shattered brow of night is bowed.
We rock beneath the oaktrees in a silver skiff.

The white walls of the city ring forever.
Beneath thorn arches,
O my brother, we blind hands climb toward midnight.

An einen Frühverstorbenen

O, der schwarze Engel, der leise aus dem Innern des Baums trat,
Da wir sanfte Gespielen am Abend waren,
Am Rand des bläulichen Brunnens.
Ruhig war unser Schritt, die runden Augen in der braunen Kühle des
      Herbstes,
O, die purpurne Süße der Sterne.

Jener aber ging die steinernen Stufen des Mönchsbergs hinab,
Ein blaues Lächeln im Antlitz und seltsam verpuppt
In seine stillere Kindheit und starb;
Und im Garten blieb das silberne Antlitz des Freundes zurück,
Lauschend im Laub oder im alten Gestein.

Seele sang den Tod, die grüne Verwesung des Fleisches
Und es war das Rauschen des Walds,
Die inbrünstige Klage des Wildes.
Immer klangen von dämmernden Türmen die blauen Glocken des
      Abends.

Stunde kam, da jener die Schatten in purpurner Sonne sah,
Die Schatten der Fäulnis in kahlem Geäst;
Abend, da an dämmernder Mauer die Amsel sang,
Der Geist des Frühverstorbenen stille im Zimmer erschien.

O, das Blut, das aus der Kehle des Tönenden rinnt,
Blaue Blume; o die feurige Träne
Geweint in die Nacht.

Goldene Wolke und Zeit. In einsamer Kammer
Lädst du öfter den Toten zu Gast,
Wandelst in trautem Gespräch unter Ulmen den grünen Fluß hinab.

To One Dead Young

O the black angel, who stepped softly from inside the tree,
When we were gentle playmates in the evening
At the edge of the bluish fountain.
Peaceful was our footstep, our eyes wide in the brown coolness of
    autumn,
O the crimson sweetness of the stars.

But he descended the stony steps of the Mönchsberg,
A blue smile on his countenance, and strangely cocooned
In his stiller childhood, and died;
And in the garden the silver countenance of the friend remained
    behind,
Listening in the foliage or in old stone.

Soul sang death, the green corruption of the flesh,
And it was the rustling of the forest,
The ardent lament of the prey.
Always the blue bells of evening rang from the dusky towers.

The hour came, when he saw shadows in the crimson sun,
Shadows of decay in the naked branches;
Evening, when the blackbird sang beside the dusky walls,
The spirit of one dead young appeared silently in the chamber.

O the blood which flows from the throat of the singer,
The blue blossom; o the fiery tears
Wept into the night.

Golden cloud and time. In a lonely chamber
Often you invite the dead one for a visit,
Beneath elms you wander closely conversing down the green river.

Geistliche Dämmerung

Stille begegnet am Saum des Waldes
Ein dunkles Wild;
Am Hügel endet leise der Abendwind,

Verstummt die Klage der Amsel,
Und die sanften Flöten des Herbstes
Schweigen im Rohr.

Auf schwarzer Wolke
Befährst du trunken von Mohn
Den nächtigen Weiher,

Den Sternenhimmel.
Immer tönt der Schwester mondene Stimme
Durch die geistliche Nacht.

Spiritual Twilight

Silently dark prey are met
At the edge of the forest;
Lightly the evening wind dies on the hill;

The plaint of the blackbird is muted,
The mild flutes of autumn
Grow still in the reeds.

On a black cloud
You sail, drunk with the poppy,
The nocturnal pond,

The starry sky.
The lunar voice of the sister rings forever
Through the spiritual night.

Abendländisches Lied

O der Seele nächtlicher Flügelschlag:
Hirten gingen wir einst an dämmernden Wäldern hin
Und es folgte das rote Wild, die grüne Blume und der lallende Quell
Demutsvoll. O, der uralte Ton des Heimchens,
Blut blühend am Opferstein
Und der Schrei des einsamen Vogels über der grünen Stille des Teichs.

O, ihr Kreuzzüge und glühenden Martern
Des Fleisches, Fallen purpurner Früchte
Im Abendgarten, wo vor Zeiten die frommen Jünger gegangen,
Kriegsleute nun, erwachend aus Wunden und Sternenträumen.
O, das sanfte Zyanenbündel der Nacht.

O, ihr Zeiten der Stille und goldener Herbste,
Da wir friedliche Mönche die purpurne Traube gekeltert;
Und rings erglänzten Hügel und Wald.
O, ihr Jagden und Schlösser; Ruh des Abends,
Da in seiner Kammer der Mensch Gerechtes sann,
In stummem Gebet um Gottes lebendiges Haupt rang.

O, die bittere Stunde des Untergangs,
Da wir ein steinernes Antlitz in schwarzen Wassern beschaun.
Aber strahlend heben die silbernen Lider die Liebenden:
Ein Geschlecht. Weihrauch strömt von rosigen Kissen
Und der süße Gesang der Auferstandenen.

Song of the West

O the nocturnal wingbeat of the soul:
Herdsmen once, we ventured along dusky forests,
And the red prey, the green flower and the murmuring spring
Modestly followed. O the primeval keen of the cricket,
Blood blossoming on the sacrificial stone,
And the cry of the lonely bird over the green silence of the pond.

O you crusades and searing torment
Of the flesh, the fall of purple fruit
In the evening garden, where pious disciples walked long ago;
Warriors now, waking from wounds and starry dreams;
O the soft cornflower-shock of the night.

O you seasons of silence and golden autumns,
When, peaceful monks, we pressed the purple clusters,
And hill and forest glimmered about us.
O you hunts and castles, repose at evening,
When man bethought justice in his chamber,
And strove in mute prayer for God's living head.

O the bitter hour of oblivion,
When we behold the stone visage in black waters.
But lovers lift their silver lids outshining:
One flesh. Incense streams from rosy cushions
And the sweet choir of the resurrected.

Verklärung

Wenn es Abend wird,
Verläßt dich leise ein blaues Antlitz.
Ein kleiner Vogel singt im Tamarindenbaum.

Ein sanfter Mönch
Faltet die erstorbenen Hände.
Ein weißer Engel sucht Marien heim.

Ein nächtiger Kranz
Von Veilchen, Korn und purpurnen Trauben
Ist das Jahr des Schauenden.

Zu deinen Füßen
Öffnen sich die Gräber der Toten,
Wenn du die Stirne in die silbernen Hände legst.

Stille wohnt
An deinem Mund der herbstliche Mond,
Trunken von Mohnsaft dunkler Gesang;

Blaue Blume,
Die leise tönt in vergilbtem Gestein.

Transfiguration

When evening comes,
A blue countenance softly leaves you.
A little bird sings in the tamarind tree.

A gentle monk
Folds the stiffened hands.
A white angel visits Mary.

The year of the watcher
Is a nocturnal wreath
Of violets, grain and purple grapes.

The graves of the dead
Open at your feet
When you lay your brow in your silver hands.

The autumn moon
Dwells silent on your mouth,
Drunk with the poppy-sap of dark song;

Blue blossom,
Which rings softly in the yellowed stone.

Föhn

Blinde Klage im Wind, mondene Wintertage,
Kindheit, leise verhallen die Schritte an schwarzer Hecke,
Langes Abendgeläut.
Leise kommt die weiße Nacht gezogen,

Verwandelt in purpurne Träume Schmerz und Plage
Des steinigen Lebens,
Daß nimmer der dornige Stachel ablasse vom verwesenden Leib.

Tief im Schlummer aufseufzt die bange Seele,

Tief der Wind in zerbrochenen Bäumen,
Und es schwankt die Klagegestalt
Der Mutter durch den einsamen Wald

Dieser schweigenden Trauer; Nächte,
Erfüllt von Tränen, feurigen Engeln.
Silbern zerschellt an kahler Mauer ein kindlich Gerippe.

Föhn

Blind lament in the wind, lunar days of winter,
Childhood, the footsteps fade softly along the black hedge,
The long knell of evening.
Softly the white night drifts in,

Transforms to crimson dreams the pain and torment
Of stony life,
That the thorny goad may not ever relent from the rotting body.

Deep in slumber sighs the fearful soul,

Deep the wind in shattered trees,
And the lament-form of the mother
Staggers through the solitary wood

Of this mute sorrow; nights,
Filled with tears, fiery angels.
Silver, an infant skeleton splinters on the naked wall.

An die Verstummten

O, der Wahnsinn der großen Stadt, da am Abend
An schwarzer Mauer verkrüppelte Bäume starren,
Aus silberner Maske der Geist des Bösen schaut;
Licht mit magnetischer Geißel die steinerne Nacht verdrängt.
O, das versunkene Läuten der Abendglocken.

Hure, die in eisigen Schauern ein totes Kindlein gebärt.
Rasend peitscht Gottes Zorn die Stirne des Besessenen,
Purpurne Seuche, Hunger, der grüne Augen zerbricht.
O, das gräßliche Lachen des Golds.

Aber stille blutet in dunkler Höhle stummere Menschheit,
Fügt aus harten Metallen das erlösende Haupt.

To Those Grown Mute

O the madness of the great city, where stunted trees
Stiffen at evening along the black wall;
The spirit of evil peers from a silver mask;
Light drives out the stony night with a magnetic scourge.
O the sunken tolling of the evening bells.

Whore, who bears a dead infant in icy shudders.
God's wrath whips raging the brow of the possessed,
Crimson plague, hunger, which shatters green eyes.
O the hideous laughter of gold.

But a muter mankind bleeds silently in a dark cavern,
Joins from hard metals the redeeming head.

Passion

Wenn Orpheus silbern die Laute rührt,
Beklagend ein Totes im Abendgarten,
Wer bist du Ruhendes unter hohen Bäumen?
Es rauscht die Klage das herbstliche Rohr,
Der blaue Teich,
Hinsterbend unter grünenden Bäumen
Und folgend dem Schatten der Schwester;
Dunkle Liebe
Eines wilden Geschlechts,
Dem auf goldenen Rädern der Tag davonrauscht.
Stille Nacht.

Unter finsteren Tannen
Mischten zwei Wölfe ihr Blut
In steinerner Umarmung; ein Goldnes
Verlor sich die Wolke über dem Steg,
Geduld und Schweigen der Kindheit.
Wieder begegnet der zarte Leichnam
Am Tritonsteich
Schlummernd in seinem hyazinthenen Haar.
Daß endlich zerbräche das kühle Haupt!

Denn immer folgt, ein blaues Wild,
Ein Äugendes unter dämmernden Bäumen,
Dieser dunkleren Pfaden
Wachend und bewegt von nächtigem Wohllaut,
Sanftem Wahnsinn;
Oder es tönte dunkler Verzückung
Voll das Saitenspiel
Zu den kühlen Füßen der Büßerin
In der steinernen Stadt.

Passion

When Orpheus silverly touches the lute,
Lamenting a death in the evening garden,
Who are you resting beneath tall trees?
The lament is rustled in the autumn reed,
The blue pond,
Dying beneath the greening trees,
And following the shadow of the sister;
Dark love
Of a wild generation,
From which the day rushes on golden wheels.
Silent night.

Beneath black firs
Two wolves mixed their blood
In an embrace of stone; the cloud
Vanished golden over the footbridge,
Patience and silence of childhood.
Again the frail corpse is seen
At Triton's pond,
Slumbering in its hyacinthine hair.
May its cool head finally shatter!

For always a blue prey,
Eyes peering beneath dusky trees,
Follows these darker paths,
Waking and moved by nocturnal sonority,
Gentle madness;
Or there sang out string music
Full of dark rapture
At cool feet of the penitent woman
In the city of stone.

Winternacht

Es ist Schnee gefallen. Nach Mitternacht verläßt du betrunken von purpurnem Wein den dunklen Bezirk der Menschen, die rote Flamme ihres Herdes. O die Finsternis!

Schwarzer Frost. Die Erde ist hart, nach Bitterem schmeckt die Luft. Deine Sterne schließen sich zu bösen Zeichen.

Mit versteinerten Schritten stampfst du am Bahndamm hin, mit runden Augen, wie ein Soldat, der eine schwarze Schanze stürmt. Avanti!

Bitterer Schnee und Mond!

Ein roter Wolf, den ein Engel würgt. Deine Beine klirren schreitend wie blaues Eis und ein Lächeln voll Trauer und Hochmut hat dein Antlitz versteinert und die Stirne erbleicht vor der Wollust des Frostes;

oder sie neigt sich schweigend über den Schlaf eines Wächters, der in seiner hölzernen Hütte hinsank.

Frost und Rauch. Ein weißes Sternenhemd verbrennt die tragenden Schultern und Gottes Geier zerfleischen dein metallenes Herz.

O der steinerne Hügel. Stille schmilzt und vergessen der kühle Leib im silbernen Schnee hin.

Schwarz ist der Schlaf. Das Ohr folgt lange den Pfaden der Sterne im Eis.

Beim Erwachen klangen die Glocken im Dorf. Aus dem östlichen Tor trat silbern der rosige Tag.

Winter Night

Snow has fallen. You leave after midnight, drunk with crimson wine, the dim precinct of men, the red flame of their hearth. O the darkness.

Black frost. The earth is hard, the air tastes of bitterness. Your stars congeal to evil signs.

With petrified footsteps you stamp along the railroad embankment, your eyes wide, like a soldier who storms a black trench. Avanti!

Bitter snow and moon!

A red wolf, which an angel strangles. Striding, your legs crackle like blue ice, and a smile full of sorrow and arrogance has petrified your countenance and blanched your brow with the lechery of frost;

or speechlessly it bends above the sleep of a sentry, who swooned away in his wooden hut.

Frost and smoke. A white shirt of stars chars the shoulders that wear it and the vultures of God flay your metallic heart.

O the stony hill. Silently the cool body dissolves, forgotten in the silver snow.

Black is your sleep. Long your ear follows the paths of the stars in the ice.

When you awoke the bells were ringing in the village. Silver, the rosy day stepped from the eastern gate.

Vorhölle

An herbstlichen Mauern, es suchen Schatten dort
Am Hügel das tönende Gold
Weidende Abendwolken
In der Ruh verdorrter Platanen.
Dunklere Tränen odmet diese Zeit,
Verdammnis, da des Träumers Herz
Überfließt von purpurner Abendröte,
Der Schwermut der rauchenden Stadt;
Dem Schreitenden nachweht goldene Kühle
Dem Fremdling, vom Friedhof,
Als folgte im Schatten ein zarter Leichnam.

Leise läutet der steinerne Bau;
Der Garten der Waisen, das dunkle Spital,
Ein rotes Schiff am Kanal.
Träumend steigen und sinken im Dunkel
Verwesende Menschen
Und aus schwärzlichen Toren
Treten Engel mit kalten Stirnen hervor;
Bläue, die Todesklagen der Mütter.
Es rollt durch ihr langes Haar,
Ein feuriges Rad, der runde Tag
Der Erde Qual ohne Ende.

Limbo

Along autumnal walls, there shadows seek
The ringing gold upon the hill,
The evening clouds, grazing
In the peace of withered sycamores.
This time breathes darker tears,
Damnation, when the dreamer's heart
Overflows with crimson sunset,
The despair of the smoky city.
Golden coolness drifts behind the walker,
The stranger, from the cemetery,
As though a frail corpse followed in the shadow.

Faintly the stone building chimes,
The garden of the orphans, the dark asylum,
A red ship on the canal.
Dreaming men, decaying,
Rise and fall in darkness,
And angels with cold brows
Step from the blackish gates;
Blue, the death-plaints of the mothers.
Through their long hair rolls
A fiery wheel, the round day
Of the earth pain without end.

In kühlen Zimmern ohne Sinn
Modert Gerät, mit knöchernen Händen
Tastet im Blau nach Märchen
Unheilige Kindheit,
Benagt die fette Ratte Tür und Truh,
Ein Herz
Erstarrt in schneeiger Stille.
Nachhallen die purpurnen Flüche
Des Hungers in faulendem Dunkel,
Die schwarzen Schwerter der Lüge,
Als schlüge zusammen ein ehernes Tor.

In cool chambers without sense
The household molders; in the blue
Unholy childhood gropes with bony hands
For fairytales,
The fat rat gnaws at door and drawer,
A heart
Grows stiff in snowy silence.
The crimson curses of hunger
Echo in the rotting darkness,
The black swords of lies,
As though a brazen gate slammed shut.

Die Sonne

Täglich kommt die gelbe Sonne über den Hügel.
Schön ist der Wald, das dunkle Tier,
Der Mensch; Jäger oder Hirt.

Rötlich steigt im grünen Weiher der Fisch.
Unter dem runden Himmel
Fährt der Fischer leise im blauen Kahn.

Langsam reift die Traube, das Korn.
Wenn sich stille der Tag neigt,
Ist ein Gutes und Böses bereitet.

Wenn es Nacht wird,
Hebt der Wanderer leise die schweren Lider;
Sonne aus finsterer Schlucht bricht.

The Sun

Daily the yellow sun comes over the hill.
Lovely is the forest, the dark beast,
Man; hunter or herdsman.

The fish rises ruddy in the green pond.
Beneath the arcing sky
The fisherman drifts quietly in a blue skiff.

The grape, the grain slowly ripen.
When the day inclines in silence,
Then a good and evil is done.

When the night comes,
Then the wanderer quietly lifts his heavy lids:
Sun breaks from a dark abyss.

Gesang einer gefangenen Amsel

Für Ludwig von Ficker

Dunkler Odem im grünen Gezweig.
Blaue Blümchen umschweben das Antlitz
Des Einsamen, den goldnen Schritt
Ersterbend unter dem Ölbaum.
Aufflattert mit trunknem Flügel die Nacht.
So leise blutet Demut,
Tau, der langsam tropft vom blühenden Dorn.
Strahlender Arme Erbarmen
Umfängt ein brechendes Herz.

Song of a Captive Blackbird

for Ludwig von Ficker

Dark breath in green branches.
Blue blossoms drift about the face
Of the lonely one, the golden footstep
Dying beneath the olive tree.
Night flutters up on a drunken wing.
Humility bleeds so softly,
Dew, dripping slowly from the blooming thorn.
The mercy of radiant arms
Embraces a breaking heart.

Abendland

Else Lasker-Schüler in Verehrung

1

Mond, als träte ein Totes
Aus blauer Höhle,
Und es fallen der Blüten
Viele über den Felsenpfad.
Silbern weint ein Krankes
Am Abendweiher,
Auf schwarzem Kahn
Hinüberstarben Liebende.

Oder es läuten die Schritte
Elis' durch den Hain
Den hyazinthenen
Wieder verhallend unter Eichen.
O des Knaben Gestalt
Geformt aus kristallenen Tränen,
Nächtigen Schatten.
Zackige Blitze erhellen die Schläfe
Die immerkühle,
Wenn am grünenden Hügel
Frühlingsgewitter ertönt.

The West

in honor of Else Lasker-Schüler

1

Moon, as though something dead
Stepped from a blue cavern,
And of the blossoms many
Fall across the rocky path.
Something sick weeps silver
At the evening pond;
On a black skiff
Lovers died across.

Or the footsteps of Elis
Ring through the grove,
The hyacinthine,
Fading again under oaktrees,
O the figure of the boy,
Formed of crystal tears,
Nocturnal shadows.
Jagged lightning lights his temples,
Ever cool,
When on the greening hill
A spring storm sounds.

2

So leise sind die grünen Wälder
Unsrer Heimat,
Die kristallene Woge
Hinsterbend an verfallner Mauer
Und wir haben im Schlaf geweint;
Wandern mit zögernden Schritten
An der dornigen Hecke hin
Singende im Abendsommer,
In heiliger Ruh
Des fern verstrahlenden Weinbergs;
Schatten nun im kühlen Schoß
Der Nacht, trauernde Adler.
So leise schließt ein mondener Strahl
Die purpurnen Male der Schwermut.

2

So quiet are the green woods
Of our homeland,
The crystal surge
Dying along the crumbled wall,
And we have wept in sleep.
Along the thorny hedge
In the evening summer
Singers wander with hesitant footsteps,
In the holy peace
Of the far-streaming vineyard;
Shadows now in the cool womb
Of the night, sorrowing eagles.
A lunar beam so softly closes
Crimson stigmata of despair.

3

Ihr großen Städte
Steinern aufgebaut
In der Ebene!
So sprachlos folgt
Der Heimatlose
Mit dunkler Stirne dem Wind,
Kahlen Bäumen am Hügel.
Ihr weithin dämmernden Ströme!
Gewaltig ängstet
Schaurige Abendröte
Im Sturmgewölk.
Ihr sterbenden Völker!
Bleiche Woge
Zerschellend am Strande der Nacht,
Fallende Sterne.

3

You great cities
Raised in stone
Upon the plain!
So speechlessly
With darkened brow
The homeless one follows the wind,
The naked trees on the hill.
You rivers glimmering in the distance!
A hideous sunset
Frightens mightily
In the stormclouds.
You dying tribes!
A pale surge
Splintering on the shore of night,
Falling stars.

Frühling der Seele

Aufschrei im Schlaf; durch schwarze Gassen stürzt der Wind,
Das Blau des Frühlings winkt durch brechendes Geäst,
Purpurner Nachttau und es erlöschen rings die Sterne.
Grünlich dämmert der Fluß, silbern die alten Alleen
Und die Türme der Stadt. O sanfte Trunkenheit
Im gleitenden Kahn und die dunklen Rufe der Amsel
In kindlichen Gärten. Schon lichtet sich der rosige Flor.

Feierlich rauschen die Wasser. O die feuchten Schatten der Au,
Das schreitende Tier; Grünendes, Blütengezweig
Rührt die kristallene Stirne; schimmernder Schaukelkahn.
Leise tönt die Sonne im Rosengewölk am Hügel.
Groß ist die Stille des Tannenwalds, die ernsten Schatten am Fluß.

Reinheit! Reinheit! Wo sind die furchtbaren Pfade des Todes,
Des grauen steinernen Schweigens, die Felsen der Nacht
Und die friedlosen Schatten? Strahlender Sonnenabgrund.

Schwester, da ich dich fand an einsamer Lichtung
Des Waldes und Mittag war und groß das Schweigen des Tiers;
Weiße unter wilder Eiche, und es blühte silbern der Dorn.
Gewaltiges Sterben und die singende Flamme im Herzen.

Dunkler umfließen die Wasser die schönen Spiele der Fische.
Stunde der Trauer, schweigender Anblick der Sonne;
Es ist die Seele ein Fremdes auf Erden. Geistlich dämmert
Bläue über dem verhauenen Wald und es läutet
Lange eine dunkle Glocke im Dorf; friedlich Geleit.
Stille blüht die Myrthe über den weißen Lidern des Toten.

Springtime of the Soul

A shriek in sleep; the wind storms through black streets,
The blue of springtime beckons through breaking branches,
Purple night-dew; and across the sky the stars go out.
The river glimmers greenly, ancient alleys silver,
And the towers of the city. O gentle drunkenness
On a gliding skiff, and the dark cries of the blackbird
In childlike gardens. Already the rosy blossoms are alight.

The waters murmur festively. O the moist shadows of the meadow,
The prancing beast; this greening, the blossoming boughs
Brush the crystal brow, the shimmer of the rocking skiff.
The sun rings softly in the roseclouds on the hill.
Great is the stillness of the firwoods, the solemn shadows on the river.

Purity! Purity! Where are the frightful paths of death,
Of gray stony silence, the rocks of the night
And the peaceless shadows? Outstreaming sun-abyss.

Sister, when I found you in the solitary clearing
Of the forest, and it was noon and great the silence of the beast;
White beneath the wild oak, and the thorn blossomed silver.
A mighty dying and the singing flame in the heart.

Darker flow the waters around the lovely play of fish.
The hour of sorrow, the silent gaze of the sun;
For the soul is a strangeness on the earth. Blue dims
Aethereally above the axe-maimed forest, and a dark bell
Long intones within the village; peaceful companionship.
Silently the myrtle blooms above the white lids of the dead.

Leise tönen die Wasser im sinkenden Nachmittag
Und es grünet dunkler die Wildnis am Ufer, Freude im rosigen Wind;
Der sanfte Gesang des Bruders am Abendhügel.

The waters ring faintly in the falling afternoon,
And on the bank the wilderness greens darker, joy in the rosy wind,
The gentle song of the brother on the evening hill.

Gesang des Abgeschiedenen

An Karl Borromaeus Heinrich

Voll Harmonien ist der Flug der Vögel. Es haben die grünen Wälder
Am Abend sich zu stilleren Hütten versammelt;
Die kristallenen Weiden des Rehs.
Dunkles besänftigt das Plätschern des Bachs, die feuchten Schatten

Und die Blumen des Sommers, die schön im Winde läuten.
Schon dämmert die Stirne dem sinnenden Menschen.

Und es leuchtet ein Lämpchen, das Gute, in seinem Herzen
Und der Frieden des Mahls; denn geheiligt ist Brot und Wein
Von Gottes Händen, und es schaut aus nächtigen Augen
Stille dich der Bruder an, daß er ruhe von dorniger Wanderschaft.
O das Wohnen in der beseelten Bläue der Nacht.

Liebend auch umfängt das Schweigen im Zimmer die Schatten der
            Alten,
Die purpurnen Martern, Klage eines großen Geschlechts,
Das fromm nun hingeht im einsamen Enkel.

Denn strahlender immer erwacht aus schwarzen Minuten des
            Wahnsinns
Der Duldende an versteinerter Schwelle
Und es umfängt ihn gewaltig die kühle Bläue und die leuchtende Neige
            des Herbstes,

Das stille Haus und die Sagen des Waldes,
Maß und Gesetz und die mondenen Pfade der Abgeschiedenen.

Song of the Departed

to Karl Borromaeus Heinrich

Full of harmonies is the flight of birds. The green woods
Have closed about the stiller huts at evening;
The crystal meadows of the stag.
Darkness soothes the plashing of the brook, the moist shadows

And the flowers of summer, ringing lovely in the wind.
Already the brow of the reflective man is dusk.

And a small lamp, kindness, is gleaming in his heart,
And the peace of the meal; for bread and wine are blessed
By the hands of God, and from nocturnal eyes the brother
Gazes silently at you, that he may rest from thorny wanderings.
O the dwelling in the soul-charged blue of night.

Lovingly the silence in the chamber clasps the shadows of the elders,
The crimson torments, the laments of a great generation,
Which is passed on devoutly in a solitary grandchild.

For out of black minutes of madness ever more radiant,
The patient one wakes on the petrified threshold,
And is ardently clasped by cool blue and the gleaming decline of the
     autumn,

The silent house and the legends of the forest,
Measure and law and the moonlit paths of the departed.

Das Herz

Das wilde Herz ward weiß am Wald;
O dunkle Angst
Des Todes, so das Gold
In grauer Wolke starb.
Novemberabend.
Am kahlen Tor am Schlachthaus stand
Der armen Frauen Schar;
In jeden Korb
Fiel faules Fleisch und Eingeweid;
Verfluchte Kost!

Des Abends blaue Taube
Brachte nicht Versöhnung.
Dunkler Trompetenruf
Durchfuhr der Ulmen
Nasses Goldlaub,
Eine zerfetzte Fahne
Vom Blute rauchend,
Daß in wilder Schwermut
Hinlauscht ein Mann.
O! ihr ehernen Zeiten
Begraben dort im Abendrot.

The Heart

The wild heart turned white at the forest;
O dark fear
Of death, as the gold
Died in a gray cloud.
November evening.
At the naked gate beside the slaughterhouse
Stood the horde of needy women;
Into each basket
Fell rotten flesh and entrails:
Accursed fare!

The blue dove of evening
Brought no atonement.
The dark blast of trumpets
Thrust through the wet
Golden foliage of the elms,
A tattered banner
Smoking with blood,
That a man lurked listening
In wild despair.
O you brazen seasons,
Buried there in sunset.

Aus dunklem Hausflur trat
Die goldne Gestalt
Der Jünglingin
Umgeben von bleichen Monden,
Herbstlicher Hofstaat,
Zerknickten schwarze Tannen
Im Nachtsturm,
Die steile Festung.
O Herz
Hinüberschimmernd in schneeige Kühle.

From the dark hallway
Stepped the golden figure
Of the maiden,
Encircled by pale moons,
Her autumnal retinue;
Black firs buckled
In the nightstorm,
The precipitous fortress.
O heart,
Shimmering over into snowy cold.

Der Schlaf

Verflucht ihr dunklen Gifte,
Weißer Schlaf!
Dieser höchst seltsame Garten
Dämmernder Bäume
Erfüllt von Schlangen, Nachtfaltern,
Spinnen, Fledermäusen.
Fremdling! Dein verlorner Schatten
Im Abendrot,
Ein finsterer Korsar
Im salzigen Meer der Trübsal.
Aufflattern weiße Vögel am Nachtsaum
Über stürzenden Städten
Von Stahl.

Sleep

Damn you dark poisons,
White sleep!
This highly peculiar garden
Of dusky trees,
Filled with serpents, nightmoths,
Spiders, bats.
Stranger! Your lost shadow
In the sunset,
A dark corsair
On the salt-seas of affliction.
White birds flap up against the seam of night
Over toppling cities
Of steel.

Der Abend

Mit toten Heldengestalten
Erfüllst du Mond
Die schweigenden Wälder,
Sichelmond—
Mit der sanften Umarmung
Der Liebenden,
Den Schatten berühmter Zeiten
Die modernden Felsen rings;
So bläulich erstrahlt es
Gegen die Stadt hin,
Wo kalt und böse
Ein verwesend Geschlecht wohnt,
Der weißen Enkel
Dunkle Zukunft bereitet.
Ihr mondverschlungnen Schatten
Aufseufzend im leeren Kristall
Des Bergsees.

The Evening

With dead shapes of heroes
You, moon, fill
The silent forests,
Sickle moon—
With the gentle embrace
Of lovers,
The shadow of times of renown,
Fill the moldering rocks all around;
So bluish it glitters
Against the city,
Where, cold and evil,
A rotting generation dwells
And prepares a dark future
For white grandchildren.
You moon-swallowed shadows,
Sighing in the empty crystal
Of the mountain lake.

Die Nacht

Dich sing ich wilde Zerklüftung,
Im Nachtsturm
Aufgetürmtes Gebirge;
Ihr grauen Türme
Überfließend von höllischen Fratzen,
Feurigem Getier,
Rauhen Farnen, Fichten,
Kristallnen Blumen.
Unendliche Qual,
Daß du Gott erjagtest
Sanfter Geist,
Aufseufzend im Wassersturz,
In wogenden Föhren.

Golden lodern die Feuer
Der Völker rings.
Über schwärzliche Klippen
Stürzt todestrunken
Die erglühende Windsbraut,
Die blaue Woge
Des Gletschers
Und es dröhnt
Gewaltig die Glocke im Tal:
Flammen, Flüche
Und die dunklen
Spiele der Wollust,
Stürmt den Himmel
Ein versteinertes Haupt.

The Night

I sing you, wild chasm,
Mountains towered up
In nightstorm;
You gray towers
Brimming with hellish grimaces,
With fiery beasts,
Bleak ferns, spruces,
Crystal blossoms.
Unending torment,
That you hunt down God,
Gentle spirit,
Sighing in the cataract,
In surging pines.

Golden flare the fires
About the tribes of men.
Above the blackish reefs
The blushing windsbride
Plunges death-drunk;
The blue surge
Of the glacier,
And the bell in the valley
Drones violently:
Flames, curses,
And the dark
Play of lust;
A stone head
Storms the sky.

Die Schwermut

Gewaltig bist du dunkler Mund
Im Innern, aus Herbstgewölk
Geformte Gestalt,
Goldner Abendstille;
Ein grünlich dämmernder Bergstrom
In zerbrochner Föhren
Schattenbezirk;
Ein Dorf,
Das fromm in braunen Bildern abstirbt.

Da springen die schwarzen Pferde
Auf nebliger Weide.
Ihr Soldaten!
Vom Hügel, wo sterbend die Sonne rollt
Stürzt das lachende Blut—
Unter Eichen
Sprachlos! O grollende Schwermut
Des Heers; ein strahlender Helm
Sank klirrend von purpurner Stirne.

Herbstesnacht so kühle kommt,
Erglänzt mit Sternen
Über zerbrochenem Männergebein
Die stille Mönchin.

Despair

Mighty are you, dark mouth,
From the inside, figure formed
Of autumn clouds
And golden evening silence;
A greenish glimmering mountain torrent
In the shadow precinct
Of shattered pines;
A village
That dies out devoutly in brown images.

There black horses leap
Upon the misty pasture.
You soldiers!
From the hill, where the sun rolls dying,
Plunges the laughing blood—
Under oaktrees,
Speechlessly! O rancorous despair
Of the army; a glittering helmet
Fell clanging from the crimson brow.

The autumn night comes on so cool;
The still monk-woman
Gleams with stars
Above the shattered limbs of men.

Im Osten

Den wilden Orgeln des Wintersturms
Gleicht des Volkes finstrer Zorn,
Die purpurne Woge der Schlacht,
Entlaubter Sterne.

Mit zerbrochnen Brauen, silbernen Armen
Winkt sterbenden Soldaten die Nacht.
Im Schatten der herbstlichen Esche
Seufzen die Geister der Erschlagenen.

Dornige Wildnis umgürtet die Stadt.
Von blutenden Stufen jagt der Mond
Die erschrockenen Frauen.
Wilde Wölfe brachen durchs Tor.

In the East

The wild organs of the winter storm
Are like the dark wrath of the tribesmen,
Like the crimson surge of battle,
Of defoliated stars.

With shattered brows and silver arms
The night beckons dying soldiers.
In the shadow of autumnal ashtrees
Sigh the spirits of the slain.

Thorny wilderness girdles the city.
The moon drives frightened women
From the bleeding steps.
Wild wolves broke through the gate.

Klage

Schlaf und Tod, die düstern Adler
Umrauschen nachtlang dieses Haupt:
Des Menschen goldnes Bildnis
Verschlänge die eisige Woge
Der Ewigkeit. An schaurigen Riffen
Zerschellt der purpurne Leib
Und es klagt die dunkle Stimme
Über dem Meer.
Schwester stürmischer Schwermut
Sieh ein ängstlicher Kahn versinkt
Unter Sternen,
Dem schweigenden Antlitz der Nacht.

Lament

Sleep and death, the somber eagles,
Rush all night about this head:
May the icy surge of eternity
Engulf the golden image
Of man. The crimson body
Shatters on the horrid reefs,
And a dark voice weeps
Above the sea.
Sister of stormy melancholy,
Look, an anxious vessel sinks
Beneath the stars,
The silent countenance of night.

Grodek

Am Abend tönen die herbstlichen Wälder
Von tödlichen Waffen, die goldnen Ebenen
Und blauen Seen, darüber die Sonne
Düstrer hinrollt; umfängt die Nacht
Sterbende Krieger, die wilde Klage
Ihrer zerbrochenen Münder.
Doch stille sammelt im Weidengrund
Rotes Gewölk, darin ein zürnender Gott wohnt
Das vergoßne Blut sich, mondne Kühle;
Alle Straßen münden in schwarze Verwesung.
Unter goldnem Gezweig der Nacht und Sternen
Es schwankt der Schwester Schatten durch den schweigenden Hain,
Zu grüßen die Geister der Helden, die blutenden Häupter;
Und leise tönen im Rohr die dunkeln Flöten des Herbstes.
O stolzere Trauer! ihr ehernen Altäre
Die heiße Flamme des Geistes nährt heute ein gewaltiger Schmerz,
Die ungebornen Enkel.

Grodek

At evening autumn forests drone
With deadly weapons, the golden plains
And the blue lakes, above which somberly
The sun rolls down. The night
Embraces dying warriors, the wild laments
Of their shattered mouths.
But in the willow valley silently
The outspilled blood collects, red clouds
In which an angry god dwells, lunar coolness;
All roads disgorge to black decay.
Beneath the golden boughs of night and stars
The sister's shadow flutters through the silent grove
To greet the spirits of the heroes, bleeding heads.
And softly in the reeds drone the dark flutes of autumn.
O prouder grief! you brazen altars;
Tonight a mighty anguish feeds the hot flame of spirit:
Unborn grandchildren.

Design by David Bullen
Typeset in Mergenthaler Berkeley Olde Style
by Wilsted & Taylor
Printed by Malloy Lithographing
on acid-free paper